the **complete** *series*

Simply salad

Published by
R&R Publications Marketing Pty Ltd
ABN 78 348 105 138
PO Box 254, Carlton North
Victoria 3054, Australia
Phone: (61 3) 9381 2199
Fax: (61 3) 9381 2689
Email: info@randrpublications.com.au
Website: www.randrpublications.com.au
Australia-wide toll-free: 1800 063 296

The Complete Salad Cookbook

Publisher: Anthony Carroll
Designer: Aisling Gallagher
Food Stylist: R&R Photstudio
Food Photography: R&R Photstudio
Recipe Development: R&R Test Kitchen

Cover recipe *Barley, feta and pear salad* on page 129

ISBN 978-1-74022-732-2

Printed September 2010
Printed in China

Contents

Introduction 4

Fish and shellfish 11

Meat and poultry 51

Grains, pulses and pasta 85

Vegetable salads 131

Mixed salads 187

Fruit salads 231

Favourite dressings 249

Index 255

Introduction

In this book you will find many delightful surprises, especially for those who thought that salads could only be served on a hot summer's day, and for those, too, who imagine a salad to be the usual greenery served time and time again.

Salads need not have a special season – simple, easy-to-prepare green salads with a special dressing or mixed vegetable salads make wonderful accompaniments to meats, chicken, fish, omelettes and quiches at any time of the year.

Whole or torn, leaves add colour and flavour to salads. Shredded, or shaped into cups for individual portions, they also play an important supporting role in the presentation of cold dishes made with other vegetables, meat, poultry or fish.

The secret to a successful salad is simple: always choose fresh, unblemished ingredients, then prepare them in an imaginative way. Combine flavours and textures carefully and always complement your salads with a compatible dressing or mayonnaise.

We know you will enjoy the salads presented in this book. You will find that the recipes contain a variety of ingredients but are simple to prepare. Fine food comes in many guises, but seldom is it as convenient, flavoursome or healthy as when it is gathered from the garden or garnered from a greengrocer with garden-fresh produce.

Fresh fruits and vegetables are relatively inexpensive, easy to prepare and full of fibre and nutrients. They come in a glorious array of colours, offer a wide range of tastes and textures and provide raw energy on a sustained level, unlike the quick gratification offered by sugary snacks.

Small wonder that salads – whether simple or carefully composed – are becoming more and more a staple of our daily diet. It is so easy to introduce raw foods in the form of a salad, either at the start of meal, as an accompaniment or, in the French fashion, as a separate course served after the main and before the dessert (to cleanse the palate and, equally importantly, to avoid any conflict between the dressing and the wine).

A hearty main-course salad can be a meal in itself, in any season. If you've never sampled a warm salad, now's the time to experience the contrast in textures and temperatures offered by Oregano lamb and couscous salad. And, while fruit salads are conventionally served as desserts, recipes like Vietnamese green papaya salad also make excellent savouries.

Knowing your greens

In recent years, the availability of various types of salad vegetables has increased so much that a trip to the greengrocer or fruit and vegetable section of any supermarket can be mind-boggling. Use the following as a guide to help you identify, and know how best to use, some of those exotic-looking salad greens.

Witlof or chicory

Sometimes called Brussels chicory or Belgian endive, this vegetable can be eaten raw or cooked. It has tightly clustered, smooth, white leaves with greenish-yellow tips and looks somewhat like an oblong tight-headed lettuce. Witlof means 'white leaf' and when buying this vegetable always look for the whitest witlof. Slightly bitter in taste, it is a versatile vegetable that combines well with a range of flavours.

Curly endive

Another member of the chicory family, curly endive has large, curly, frilly-edged leaves with a slightly bitter flavour. The leaves graduate from a pale, green yellow to dark green. Use the paler heart leaves and stalks. Sold in large bunches, curly endive makes an attractive bed for a meat or chicken salad and is an interesting addition to a mixed green salad.

Butter or round lettuce

There are a several varieties of butter lettuce, including bibb, Boston and butterhead. The one thing they have in common is that they are a soft, smallish lettuce with a mild flavour. Often grown hydroponically, the butter lettuce lacks the crunch of iceberg or cos, but is popular in mixed lettuce salads.

Cos or romaine lettuce

Popular with the Romans, this lettuce was named by them because they claim to have discovered it on the Greek island of Cos. Later the English and Europeans renamed it romaine lettuce after the Romans. Today it is known by both names, depending on where in the world you reside. This lettuce has an elongated head of dark green oval leaves and a crisp pale green heart. It has a pungent flavour and stays crisp. Its main claim to fame is its use in the traditional Caesar Salad.

Iceberg or crisp head lettuce

Probably the most popular and well, known of lettuces, the iceberg lettuce is a large lettuce with crisp outer leaves and a firm, sweet heart. It is the basis of many salads as it combines well with other lettuces and salad greens.

Red leaf lettuces

These are among the prettiest of lettuces and include mignonette, lollo rosso and red oakleaf. They are characterised by their soft, smallish leaves with pink- to red-tinged edges. These lettuces have a delicate sweet flavour. The red leaf lettuces are usually interchangeable in a recipe and more often than not are used to give a salad colour and interest.

Radicchio

Yet another member of the chicory family, radicchio is beetroot-coloured with white veins and has a tightly packed head. It has a tangy, slightly bitter flavour and is a much–loved salad vegetable in Italy, where it is called red chicory. In Italy, radicchio is the name generally used for chicory.

Rocket

Also known as arugula, roquette and rugula, this plant has small, peppery, dark green leaves and should be used while still young. Rocket first grew wild in the Mediterranean area and was a popular salad green with the ancient Romans. Still rare in many areas, it is in fact easy to grow and for something different in your salads, it is well worth the effort.

English spinach or spinach

The young, fresh, dark green leaves of this vegetable are delicious eaten raw. One of the most popular spinach salads consists of roughly torn spinach leaves, crisp bacon pieces and croutons, with a dressing made from lemon juice, freshly ground black pepper and the cooking juices of the bacon.

Watercress

Watercress has smooth round leaves, crunchy stems and a pungent, slightly peppery flavour. Use young outer leaves and tender stems for salads. The remainder can be used in soups. Watercress has long been used as both a food and a medicine and can be traced back to the ancient Greeks. It combines well with other milder salad greens and is popular as a garnish for salads and open sandwiches. Watercress does not keep well and should be stored upright in the refrigerator in a container of water, and covered with a plastic food bag. Change the water daily to ensure lasting freshness.

Salad vegetables

While lettuce, chicory and a variety of other greens form the basis of many salads, there are also a number of other salad vegetables that are popular and should not be forgotten.

Cabbage

One of the oldest cultivated vegetable species, the cabbage family includes white cabbage, red cabbage and yellow and green Savoy cabbage. Used raw and finely shredded, it is the basis of the ever-popular coleslaw. Red cabbage, usually cooked, is also delicious raw, and when shredded and combined with green cabbage makes an attractive slaw. Store cabbage in a plastic food bag in the crisper section of the refrigerator.

Red, green or yellow capsicum

Also called peppers and bell peppers, when sliced or chopped these add colour and crunch to salads. Always choose well-shaped, firm capsicums with a glossy, smooth skin. Dull-looking capsicums, and those with soft spots and wrinkled skins should be avoided. Remove the stalk, seeds and white membrane before use. Roasted capsicum also makes an interesting salad garnish. Capsicums should keep in the crisper section of the refrigerator for 5–7 days.

Celery

Use either sliced, cut into sticks or as celery curls. The leaves also make a tasty and attractive salad garnish.

Cucumber

The variety of cucumbers available include apple, green or ridge, Lebanese and Continental. The green or ridge and Continental cucumbers are the most widely available. To prepare cucumbers, you need only peel them if the skin is tough or bitter, as leaving the skin on is said to help with digestion. Cucumbers (except the apple variety) should have bright green skins with a firm, fresh appearance. Apple cucumbers should have a pale yellow-white skin.

Onions

All types of onions can be used raw in salads. White and brown onions have a strong, hot, pungent taste and should be used sparingly. The red onion is a mild sweet onion that adds a pretty colour to any salad. Spring onions, also known as scallions or green onions, give a mild fresh onion flavour. Use onions either sliced or chopped in salads or as a garnish.

Radishes

These small, crisp red bulbs can be used whole, sliced, chopped or grated in salads. Select radishes with fresh-looking leaves and bright-coloured bulbs.

Sprouts

There are a number of sprout varieties available, the most popular being alfalfa and bean sprouts. Sprouts should be kept in a plastic food bag or the container in which you purchased them.

Tomatoes

Tomatoes should have a good red colour and firm flesh. Used whole or halved, cherry and yellow teardrop tomatoes are also popular salad ingredients. For best flavour, tomatoes should always be used at room temperature.

Hydroponically grown lettuces last longer, as they are still growing when you buy them and will continue to grow if kept in a plastic food bag in the crisper section of the refrigerator. Many varieties are now grown hydroponically, making them available all year round.

Lettuce should be stored in the vegetable crisper section of your refrigerator. Place the whole lettuce in a plastic food bag or covered container. Separate leaves and wash just prior to using.

To prepare lettuce, cut out the core using a stainless steel knife, then separate leaves and wash briefly in cold water. Dry the leaves by shaking off the excess water, then pat dry with a tea towel. The leaves can also be drained in a colander or salad basket, or use a salad spinner or centrifugal dryer (a piece of equipment especially designed for drying lettuce leaves).

Always dress a lettuce salad as close to serving time as possible– the longer the dressing sits on the leaves, the less crisp they will be.

fish and shellfish

A salad book such as this one is full of vegetable-based recipes, as it should be. However, for the sake of balance, we have included this chapter of fish and shellfish salads. Artfully arranged, they will satisfy the eye, please the appetite and delight those participating in the meal. In addition, seafood ranks very highly in the nutrition stakes.

Fijian kokoda

2½lb/1¼ kg firm white fish
1 cup fresh lime or lemon juice
10 oz/300mL canned coconut milk
salt and freshly ground black pepper
1 small red capsicum, finely diced
1 small green capsicum, finely diced
1 small red chilli, minced
1 firm tomato, finely diced
lime or lemon wedges

1 Cut the fish into ½ in/12mm cubes and mix with 7 oz/200mL of the lime juice, half the coconut milk, and salt and pepper to taste. Stir well and marinate for 4 hours.

2 When the fish is firm and looks opaque (cooked), drain away and discard the liquid.

3 Mix the drained fish with the capsicum pieces, chilli and tomato. Add the remaining coconut milk and lime juice and stir to combine thoroughly.

4 Serve cold in glasses with wedges of lime or lemon as an entrée.

Serves 4 • Preparation 4 hours 15 minutes

Marinated salmon, cucumber and daikon salad

1½ lb/700g fillet of salmon, centre-cut
6 tablespoons mirin (sweet Japanese rice wine)
3 tablespoons Japanese soy sauce
2 in/5cm piece ginger, grated
1 teaspoon toasted sesame oil
1 Continental cucumber
1 teaspoon sea salt
1 tablespoon caster sugar
3 tablespoons rice vinegar
curly endive, well washed and dried
1 daikon (white radish), finely julienned

1 Ask your fishmonger to slice the salmon thinly, as for smoked salmon. If they can't or won't, have the skin removed and slice the salmon into very thin strips – if you feel you are able to slice the salmon on an angle this would be desirable, but if not, cut straight down.

2 Whisk the mirin, soy, ginger and sesame oil together, then remove 2 tablespoons and reserve. Pour the remainder into a shallow bowl and add the sliced salmon fillet, allowing the fish to marinate for 2 hours.

3 Meanwhile, peel the cucumber and, using a vegetable peeler or food slicer, cut the cucumber into long, thin slices and place these in a bowl. Mix together the sea salt, sugar and rice vinegar and drizzle over the cucumber, tossing well to coat the slices in the dressing.

4 Arrange slices of marinated salmon on the plates then place the curly endive and white radish in the centre. Weave some drained cucumber slices through the salad then drizzle a little of the reserved mirin dressing over the salad.

Serves 6 • Preparation 2 hours

Caramelised ocean trout salad with cellophane noodles

2 tablespoons olive oil
10 French shallots, chopped
7 oz/200g brown sugar
3½ oz/100mL fish sauce
3 in/8cm piece fresh ginger, julienned
10 small chillies, halved, seeds removed and julienned
2 tablespoons lime juice
7 oz/200g cellophane noodles
1 bunch fresh coriander leaves, chopped
1 lb/500g ocean trout fillets, cut into 1 in/25mm-thick strips

1 Heat the olive oil and gently sauté the chopped shallots until golden. Add the sugar and heat in the pan until the sugar has dissolved. Cook on a medium heat until the mixture has caramelised, about 5 minutes, stir well. Add the fish sauce, ginger, chillies and lime juice and stir well until combined. Keep hot.

2 Soak the cellophane noodles in hot water until they have softened, about 10 minutes, then refresh in cold water. Drain, then add the coriander leaves and just enough of the sauce to moisten the noodles.

3 Meanwhile, pan-fry or grill the fish fillets until just cooked.

4 Arrange the noodles on individual plates then place the fish pieces decoratively on top. Garnish with extra chillies and coriander leaves and spoon more sauce over.

If you want the dish to be extra hot, then simple halve the chillies and leave the seeds inside.

Serves 4 • Preparation 35 minutes • Cooking 15 minutes

Thai calamari salad

3 calamari tubes, cleaned
6 oz/185g green beans, sliced lengthwise
2 tomatoes, cut into wedges
1 small green pawpaw, peeled, deseeded and shredded
4 spring onions, sliced
1 oz/30g fresh mint leaves
1 oz/30g fresh coriander leaves
1 fresh red chilli, chopped

Lime dressing
2 teaspoons brown sugar
3 tablespoons lime juice
1 tablespoon fish sauce

1 Using a sharp knife, make a single cut down the length of each calamari tube and open out. Cut parallel lines down the length of the calamari, taking care not to cut right the way through the flesh. Make more cuts in the opposite direction to form a diamond pattern.
2 Heat a non stick chargrill or frying pan over a high heat, add calamari and cook for 1–2 minutes each side or until tender. Remove from pan and cut into thin strips.
3 Place calamari, beans, tomatoes, pawpaw, spring onions, mint, coriander and chilli in a serving bowl.
4 To make dressing, place sugar, lime juice and fish sauce in a screw-top jar and shake well. Drizzle over salad and toss to combine. Cover and stand for 20 minutes before serving.

Serves 4 • Preparation 30 minutes • Cooking 10 minutes

Seared scallop salad

2 teaspoons oil
2 cloves garlic, crushed
13 oz/375g scallops, cleaned
4 rashers bacon, chopped
1 cos lettuce, leaves separated
2 oz/60g croutons
1 oz/30g Parmesan cheese

Mustard dressing
3 tablespoons mayonnaise
1 tablespoon olive oil
1 teaspoon sesame oil
1 tablespoon vinegar
2 teaspoons Dijon mustard

1 To make dressing, place mayonnaise, olive oil, sesame oil, vinegar and mustard in a bowl, mix to combine and set aside.
2 Heat oil in a frying pan over a high heat, add garlic and scallops and cook, stirring, for 1 minute or until scallops just turn opaque. Remove scallop mixture from pan and set aside. Add bacon to pan and cook, stirring, for 4 minutes or until crisp. Remove bacon from pan and drain on absorbent paper.
3 Place lettuce leaves in a large salad bowl, add dressing and toss to coat. Add bacon, croutons and shavings of Parmesan cheese and toss to combine. Spoon scallop mixture over salad and serve.

Serves 2 • Preparation 10 minutes • Cooking 8 minutes

Salmon and lentil salad

1 cos lettuce, leaves separated and torn into large pieces
7 oz/200g green lentils, cooked and drained
7 oz/200g red lentils, cooked and drained
8 oz/250g cherry tomatoes, halved
5 oz/150g wholemeal croutons
1 tablespoon chilli oil or vegetable oil
13 oz/375g salmon fillets, skin removed, cut into 3cm-wide strips
1 oz/30g Parmesan cheese
freshly ground black pepper

Dressing
½ cup mayonnaise
2 tablespoons vegetable stock
1 tablespoon wholegrain mustard
1 tablespoon white wine vinegar

1 To make dressing, place mayonnaise, stock, mustard and vinegar in a bowl and mix to combine. Set aside.

2 Arrange lettuce, cooked lentils, tomatoes and croutons attractively on a serving platter. Set aside.

3 Heat oil in a frying pan over a medium heat, add salmon and cook, turning several times, for 4 minutes or until salmon is cooked. Remove from pan and arrange on top of salad. Drizzle dressing over salad and top with shavings of Parmesan cheese and black pepper to taste.

Serves 4 • Preparation 15 minutes • Cooking 5 minutes

Chickpea and trout salad

1 bunch curly endive, leaves separated
1 bunch rocket
14 oz/400g canned chickpeas, rinsed and drained
4 oz/125g herbed goat's cheese, crumbled
1 red onion, sliced
8 oz/250g smoked trout, skin and bones removed, flesh flaked
¼ cup fresh basil, chopped
1 red capsicum, halved, roasted, skin removed and flesh sliced

Honey lime dressing
½ cup plain yoghurt
¼ cup fresh mint, chopped
1 tablespoon ground cumin
1 tablespoon honey
1 tablespoon lime juice

1 Arrange the endive and rocket on a serving platter. Top with the chickpeas, cheese, onion and trout. Sprinkle the salad with basil and top with capsicum.

Honey lime dressing

1 Place the yoghurt, mint, cumin, honey and lime juice in a bowl and mix to combine. Drizzle the dressing over the salad and serve immediately.

Chickpeas are slightly crunchy and lend a nutty flavour to salads, casseroles, soups and other savoury dishes. Dried chickpeas can be used instead of canned. To cook dried chickpeas, soak overnight in cold water. Drain. Place in a large saucepan, cover with cold water and bring to the boil over a medium heat. Reduce the heat and simmer for 45–60 minutes or until the chickpeas are tender. Drain and cool.

Serves 4 • Preparation 20 minutes

Honeyed calamari salad

6 small calamari, cleaned and sliced into rings
½ cup plain flour
olive oil for shallow-frying
lettuce leaves of your choice
8 oz/250g cherry tomatoes, halved
1 onion, thinly sliced

Honey orange dressing
¼ cup olive oil
1 tablespoon orange juice
1 tablespoon vinegar
1 teaspoon honey
1 clove garlic, crushed
½ teaspoon mild mustard
freshly ground black pepper

1 Dry the calamari on absorbent paper. Toss them in flour and shake off the excess.
   Heat the oil in a frying pan over a medium heat, add the calamari and stir-fry for
   1–2 minutes or until golden. Drain on absorbent paper.

2 Place the lettuce leaves, tomatoes and onion in a bowl and toss. Divide the lettuce
   mixture among serving plates, top with the hot calamari and drizzle with dressing.
   Serve immediately.

Honey orange dressing

1 To make the dressing, place the oil, orange juice, vinegar, honey, garlic, mustard and
   black pepper in a screw-top jar and shake well to combine.

**To clean fresh calamari, pull off the tentacles, carefully taking with them the head,
stomach and ink bag. Rub off the skin under cold running water. Slice the tube (body)
crosswise into rings. If fresh calamari is unavailable, use 12 oz/340g frozen calamari
rings instead.**

Serves 4 • Preparation 25 minutes • Cooking 2 minutes

Peach and prawn entrée salad

7 oz/200g dried peaches
1 tablespoon lemon juice
grated zest of 1 lemon
2 teaspoons brown sugar
½ teaspoon salt
½ teaspoon freshly ground black pepper
⅓ cup sherry vinegar
2 drops Tabasco
2 teaspoons Dijon mustard
1 egg
⅔ cup light olive oil
1 lb/500g green salad leaves
12 cooked king prawns, shelled and deveined

1 Place the peaches in a flat dish. Mix the lemon juice, zest, brown sugar, salt, pepper, vinegar and Tabasco together and pour over the peaches. Allow to stand at room temperature for 30 minutes.

2 Remove the peaches from the vinegar mixture. Pour the vinegar mixture into a blender or food processor, add the mustard and egg, and process until smooth. With the motor running, add the oil in a thin, steady stream. The dressing will become creamy and thicken slightly.

3 Divide the salad mix among 4 plates, place 2 peach halves on top of the salad and arrange 3 prawns on each plate. Spoon the dressing over the salad and serve immediately.

Serves 4 • Preparation 45 minutes

Lobster and smoked ocean trout salad

1 cooked lobster tail
14 oz/400g smoked ocean trout
1 Continental cucumber
1 carrot, peeled
1 green zucchini
1 yellow zucchini
3½ oz/100g tatsoi leaves
1 bunch chives, chopped
Dressing
juice of 2 limes
1 tablespoon palm sugar
½ cup olive oil
salt and freshly ground black pepper

1 Remove the meat from the lobster's tail, slice finely and set aside. Alternatively, ask your fishmonger to do this for you. Cut the trout into thin strips and also set aside.

2 Slice the cucumber in half lengthwise and scoop out and discard the seeds. Slice on a mandoline or 'V-slicer' (or use a vegetable peeler) to make long, skinny strips resembling fettuccine. Slice in the same way as the cucumber. Slice the zucchini lengthwise into long thin strips.

3 Mix the lobster, trout, vegetables and tatsoi leaves gently.

4 For the dressing, heat the lime juice and dissolve the palm sugar in it. Pour into a bowl and whisk in the olive oil until the mixture is thick and the oil has emulsified with the lime juice. Season with salt and pepper and mix the dressing through the salad ingredients.

5 Arrange the salad on an attractive platter and sprinkle over the chives.

Serves 6–8 • Preparation 40 minutes

Prawn and avocado cocktail

14 oz/400g cooked peeled prawns, defrosted if frozen
8 tablespoons mayonnaise
4 tablespoons tomato sauce
2 stalks celery, finely chopped
1 green onion, finely sliced
salt and freshly ground black pepper
2 avocados
1 tablespoon lemon juice

1 Mix together the prawns, mayonnaise and tomato sauce in a bowl, then stir in the celery and onion and season to taste.
2 Halve the avocados, remove the stones and peel. Dice the flesh, then toss in the lemon juice to stop it browning. Add to the prawn mixture, stirring lightly, then transfer to glasses or serving plates and grind over a little extra pepper.

A classic starter that's even better when you add chunks of ripe avocado.
This gives 4 generous portions, so you can also serve it with crisp leaves as a salad.

Serves 4 • Preparation 15 minutes

Mixed shellfish and potato salad

1½ lb/750g waxy potatoes, unpeeled
4 small cooked beetroots, diced
1 head fennel, finely sliced, plus feathery
  top, chopped
2 lb/1 kg mussels
1 lb/500g clams
10 oz/300mL dry white wine or cider
1 French shallot, finely chopped
4 green onions, finely sliced
¼ cup fresh parsley, chopped

Dressing
2½ oz/75mL olive oil
1 tablespoon cider vinegar
1 teaspoon English mustard
salt and freshly ground black pepper

1 Boil the potatoes in salted water for 15 minutes or until tender, then drain. Cool for 30 minutes, then peel and slice.

2 Meanwhile, make the dressing by whisking together the oil, vinegar, mustard and seasoning.

3 Place the potatoes in a bowl and toss with half the dressing. Toss the beetroots and fennel with the rest of the dressing.

4 Scrub the mussels and clams under cold running water, pulling away any beards from the mussels. Discard any shellfish that are open or damaged. Place the wine or cider and French shallot in a large saucepan and bring to the boil. Simmer for 2 minutes, then add the shellfish. Cover and cook briskly for 3–5 minutes, shaking the pan often, until the shellfish have opened. Discard any that remain closed. Reserve the pan juices, set aside a few mussels in their shells and shell the rest.

5 Boil the pan juices for 5 minutes or until reduced to ½–1 oz/15–25mL. Strain over the potatoes. Add the shellfish flesh, green onions and parsley, then toss. Serve with the beetroot and fennel salad and garnish with the fennel tops and reserved mussels in their shells.

Serves 4 • Preparation 45 minutes • Cooking 30 minutes

Tuna bean salad

8 oz/250g dried haricot beans
1 onion, halved
15 oz/425g canned tuna, drained and flaked
3 spring onions, chopped
1 red capsicum, diced
½ cup fresh parsley, chopped
3 tablespoons olive oil
2 tablespoons cider vinegar
freshly ground black pepper

1 Place beans in a large bowl, cover with water and set aside to soak overnight, then drain. Place beans and onion in a saucepan with enough water to cover and bring to the boil. Boil for 10 minutes, then reduce heat and simmer for 1 hour or until beans are tender. Remove onion and discard, drain beans and set aside to cool.

2 Place beans, tuna, spring onions, capsicum and parsley in a salad bowl.

3 Place oil, vinegar and black pepper in a screw-top jar and shake well to combine. Pour dressing over bean mixture and toss to combine. Serve immediately.

Serves 4 • Preparation 20 minutes plus soaking time • Cooking 1 hour 10 minutes

Tuna and lemon fettuccine salad

1 lb/500g fettuccine
15 oz/425g canned tuna in spring water, drained and flaked
7 oz/200g rocket leaves, roughly chopped
5 oz/150g feta cheese, chopped
4 sprigs dill, chopped
¼ cup lemon juice
freshly ground black pepper

1 Bring a large saucepan of salted water to the boil, add the fettuccine and cook for 8 minutes or until just firm in the centre (al dente). Drain and return pasta to the saucepan.

2 Place the saucepan over a low heat and add tuna, rocket, feta, dill, lemon juice and black pepper to taste. Toss to combine, and serve immediately.

Serves 4 • Preparation 10 minutes • Cooking 8 minutes

Barbecued seafood salad

2 tablespoons lemon juice
1 tablespoon olive oil
10 oz/300g firm white fish such as swordfish, mackerel or cod, cut into 1 in/25mm cubes
10 oz/300g pink fish such as salmon, marlin or tuna, cut into 1 in/25mm cubes
12 scallops
12 raw prawns (with or without shell)
1 calamari tube, cut into rings
1 bunch watercress, broken into sprigs
1 large red onion, cut into rings
1 long cucumber, peeled and thinly sliced

Raspberry and tarragon dressing
3 sprigs tarragon, leaves removed and stalks discarded
2 tablespoons raspberry or red wine vinegar
2 tablespoons lemon juice
1 tablespoon olive oil
freshly ground black pepper

1 Place lemon juice and oil in a bowl. Whisk to combine. Add white and pink fish, scallops, prawns and calamari. Toss to combine. Cover and marinate in the refrigerator for 1 hour or until ready to use (do not marinate for longer than 2 hours).

2 For the dressing, place tarragon, vinegar, lemon juice, oil and black pepper in a screw-top jar. Shake to combine and set aside.

3 Preheat a barbecue or grill until very hot. Line a serving platter with watercress. Drain seafood mixture and place on barbecue plate or in pan. Add onion and cook, turning several times, for 6–8 minutes or until seafood is just cooked. Take care not to overcook or the seafood will be tough and dry.

4 Transfer seafood to a bowl. Add cucumber and dressing. Toss to combine. Spoon seafood mixture over watercress and serve immediately.

Serves 8 • Preparation 1 hour 20 minutes • Cooking 10 minutes

Scandinavian mussels

2 lb/1kg mussels, cleaned
1 small onion, sliced
1 stalk celery, sliced
1 clove garlic, chopped
¼ cup white wine
4 tablespoons mayonnaise
½ cup parsley, chopped
juice of 1 lemon
salt and freshly ground black pepper

Vegatables
½ onion, finely chopped
½ stalk celery, finely chopped
½ red capsicum, finely chopped
1 tablespoon sugar
1 tablespoon white wine vinegar

1 Put mussels in a casserole with onion, celery, garlic and wine. Cook until mussels have opened, stirring frequently to make sure mussels are cooked evenly. Discard vegetables and remove mussels from their shells.

2 To make the vegetables, combine ½ cup water, the onion, celery, red capsicum, sugar and vinegar in a small saucepan and boil for 1 minute. Remove vegetables from liquid and set aside to cool. Discard liquid.

3 Mix mussels, mayonnaise, vegetables, parsley and lemon juice in a bowl, and add salt and pepper to taste. Serve cold with a green salad or a cold potato salad and decorated with a few mussel shells.

Serves 2 • Preparation 20 minutes • Cooking 15 minutes

Garlic prawn salad

1 tablespoon extra virgin olive oil
4 cloves garlic, crushed
½ teaspoon chilli flakes
24 large raw prawns, shelled and deveined
1 medium tomato, sliced
1 cos lettuce, outer leaves discarded
1 Lebanese cucumber, sliced into ribbons
salt and freshly ground black pepper
juice of 1 lime
juice of 1 lemon

1 Heat a large heavy-based frying pan, add the oil, garlic, chilli flakes and prawns.
   Cook, stirring constantly, until the prawns change colour, about 3 minutes.
2 Divide the tomato slices between 4 serving plates, top with lettuces leaves and
   cucumber ribbons. Add the prawns and pour over the pan juices. Season with salt
   and pepper, then squeeze over the lemon and lime juices and serve.

Serves 4 • Preparation 12 minutes • Cooking 4 minutes

Mediterranean scallop salad

1 tablespoon olive oil
7 oz/200g small prawns, peeled
7 oz/200g scallops
3 lettuces, cut into ribbons
2 large red onions, sliced

Dressing
2 tablespoons Dijon mustard
zest and juice of 2 limes
5 tablespoons Greek yoghurt
2 teaspoons tomato paste
1 red chilli, deseeded and finely chopped
4 tablespoons extra virgin olive oil
½ cup fresh dill or mint, chopped
pinch of salt

1 Heat the oil in a medium frying pan over a medium heat and fry the prawns and scallops for 4 minutes until just cooked. Set aside to cool.
2 To make the dressing, place the mustard, lime juice, yoghurt, tomato paste and chilli in a bowl and mix well. Whisk in the oil, a little at a time, then stir in the dill or mint and lime zest and season with salt.
3 Place the lettuce in a salad bowl, arrange the seafood and onion rings on top and drizzle over the dressing. Garnish with extra dill or mint.

Serves 4 • Preparation 10 minutes • Cooking 4 minutes

Baby octopus salad

12 baby octopuses
2 teaspoons coriander seeds, toasted
2 cloves garlic, finely minced, plus 12 cloves, sliced
2 tablespoons lemon juice
4 tablespoons sweet chilli sauce
2 Continental cucumbers
1 large red capsicum
1 bunch watercress
1 cup pickled ginger
1 tablespoon black sesame seeds
1 cup coriander leaves
1 cup bean sprouts
1 cup canola oil

1 Clean octopuses by peeling off skin and removing heads. Grind coriander seeds in a mortar and pestle. Combine coriander seeds, minced garlic, lemon juice and sweet chilli sauce in bowl. Add octopus and marinate in refrigerator for 2 hours.

2 Using a vegetable peeler, peel thin strips of cucumber. Thinly slice capsicum lengthwise. Combine watercress, cucumber, capsicum, pickled ginger, sesame seeds, coriander leaves and bean sprouts in a large bowl. Set aside.

3 Heat oil in a frying pan and fry sliced garlic until golden brown and crispy. Remove and drain on absorbent paper.

4 Strain marinade from the octopus into a small saucepan and bring to simmer. Set aside to cool and use as dressing later. Heat a wok and stir-fry octopus until cooked, approximately 3–4 minutes.

5 Combine prepared salad with octopus and toss through dressing. Serve garnished with crispy garlic.

Serves 4 • Preparation 2 hours 30 minutes • Cooking 10 minutes

meat and poultry

As the trend towards lighter eating continues, salads are becoming increasingly popular as main meals. The salads we offer in this chapter are mainly one-dish meals–try the Summer salad of grilled chicken, spinach and mango or Salad of sautéed duck with thyme and honey to start with.

Summer salad of grilled chicken, spinach and mango

6 Roma tomatoes
10 basil leaves, sliced
10 mint leaves, sliced
salt and freshly ground black pepper
½ teaspoon sugar
12 tenderloins chicken
1 bunch asparagus
1 avocado
1 bunch spring onions
8 firm button mushrooms
2 firm mangoes
3 handfuls baby spinach leaves
½ cup toasted hazelnuts, lightly crushed
½ cup toasted Brazil nuts, lightly crushed

½ cup toasted pistachios, lightly crushed

Dressing
2 teaspoons honey
2 tablespoons balsamic vinegar
3 tablespoons raspberry vinegar
2 tablespoons soy sauce
2 teaspoons Dijon mustard
2cm piece ginger, minced
2 cloves garlic, minced
1 teaspoon sambal oelek (chilli paste)
2 tablespoons lemon juice
2 tablespoons olive oil
salt and freshly ground black pepper

1 Preheat the oven to 320°F/160°C. Slice the tomatoes in half lengthwise, and top with sliced basil, mint, salt, pepper and sugar. Bake for 2 hours, then cut into quarters.

2 In a large jug, whisk together all the dressing ingredients until emulsified (thickened).

3 Marinate the chicken in ½ cup of dressing, reserving the remainder for later. Allow the chicken to marinate for 1 hour minimum (or up to 4 hours). Heat a non-stick grill pan and cook the chicken over a high heat until cooked through, 2–3 minutes on each side. Transfer the cooked chicken to a plate and keep warm.

4 Steam the asparagus until tender then refresh under cold water. Halve the avocado, peel, and dice the flesh. Slice the spring onions diagonally and thinly slice the mushrooms. Dice the mango flesh.

5 To make the salad, place the well-washed spinach leaves in a large bowl and add the asparagus, spring onions, mushrooms and roasted tomatoes. Add the reserved dressing and toss thoroughly.

6 Divide the salad evenly amongst six individual plates and add the mango and avocado cubes. Top each with 2 chicken tenderloins, and a generous sprinkling of nuts. Serve immediately.

Serves 6 • Preparation 1 hour 30 minutes • Cooking 2 hours 20 minutes

Salad of sautéed duck with thyme and honey

3 duck breasts, skin on
salt and freshly ground black pepper
1 tablespoon peanut oil
2 teaspoons butter
2 sprigs thyme
2 tablespoons honey
1 tablespoon lemon juice
2 tablespoons walnut oil
7 oz/200g mixed baby lettuce leaves, washed and spun dry
6 large cherry tomatoes
¼ cup basil leaves

1 Heat the oven to 380°F/190°C. Season duck breast with a little salt and pepper.

2 Heat peanut oil in a pan until almost smoking then add the duck breast, skin-side down, and cook on a high heat until the skin is deep caramel brown. Transfer the pan containing the duck to the preheated oven until the duck is cooked rare, about 7–10 minutes. Do not turn the duck breasts over.

3 Remove the pan from the oven and remove the breasts from pan, keeping them warm, and drain and discard the excess fat. Add the butter, and when it begins to bubble, add the thyme then the honey. When simmering, replace duck breasts, skin-side up.

4 Cook for a further minute on low heat then remove from the pan altogether.

5 Whisk together the lemon juice, walnut oil, salt and pepper and the pan juices and mix well. Toss the lettuce leaves through a little of the dressing.

6 Divide the lettuce leaves between the plates, garnish with tomatoes. Slice duck breast and arrange around the salad, drizzling any excess honey sauce over the duck slices. Garnish with basil leaves and serve.

Serves 4 • Preparation 25 minutes • Cooking 20 minutes

Italian chicken salad

3 chicken breast fillets, all visible fat and skin removed
olive oil
4 oz/125g baby spinach leaves
4 oz/125g green beans, blanched
1 red onion, thinly sliced
2 tablespoons small capers, drained

Vinegar and prune dressing
8 pitted prunes
1 tablespoon fresh oregano leaves
zest of 1 lemon
1 teaspoon sugar
½ cup red wine vinegar

1 Heat a non-stick chargrill or frying pan over a high heat. Lightly oil chicken, add to pan and cook for 2–3 minutes each side or until tender. Remove from pan and set aside to cool.
2 To make dressing, place prunes, oregano, lemon zest, sugar and vinegar in a saucepan over a low heat, bring to simmering and simmer for 5 minutes.
3 To assemble salad, cut chicken breasts into thin slices. Arrange spinach, beans, onion, chicken and capers attractively on serving plates. Drizzle a little warm dressing over the salad and serve immediately. Serve any remaining dressing separately.

Serves 4 • Preparation 15 minutes • Cooking 20 minutes

Asian chicken bok choy salad

8 fresh or dried shiitake mushrooms
⅓ oz/10g black cloud ear fungus
28 oz/800g cooked chicken, skin off, shredded
2 lb/1kg fresh Asian noodles
7 oz/200g fresh snowpeas, diagonally sliced
4 baby bok choy, well washed and leaves separated
1 red capsicum, diced
4 spring onions, finely sliced
8 oz/250g canned sliced water chestnuts, drained

2 in/4cm piece fresh ginger, minced
¼ cup natural yoghurt
3 tablespoons kecap manis
1 tablespoon hoisin sauce
3 tablespoons mirin
3 tablespoons rice vinegar
3 tablespoons sweet chilli sauce
1 tablespoon fish sauce
juice of 1 lime
salt and freshly ground black pepper
2 tablespoons slivered almonds, toasted
1 bunch chervil, parsley or coriander

1 If using dried shiitake, soak in hot water for 15 minutes then drain and slice. If using fresh shiitake, slice finely. Soak the black cloud ear fungus for 15 minutes then drain. Rinse the soaked mushrooms thoroughly in cold water.

2 Place the shredded cooked chicken in a large bowl. Pour boiling hot water over the noodles until they have separated then shake off excess water and add the noodles to the chicken. Add the mushrooms, snowpeas, baby bok choy leaves, capsicum, spring onions and water chestnuts and toss well.

3 In a jug, whisk together the ginger, yoghurt, kecap manis, hoisin, mirin, rice vinegar, sweet chilli, fish sauce, lime juice and salt and pepper to taste. Add to the chicken salad and toss very well until all the ingredients are coated. Garnish with the toasted slivered almonds and chopped chervil, parsley or coriander and serve.

Dried shiitake mushrooms and black cloud ear fungus are both available from Asian grocery stores.

Serves 6–8 • Preparation 40 minutes

New Mexico chicken salad

1 bunch young rocket
edible flowers of your choice
6 radicchio leaves, shredded
1 grapefruit, peeled with all white pith removed, segmented
2 smoked chicken breasts, sliced

Pine nut and chilli dressing
4 tablespoons pine nuts, toasted
6 bay leaves
2 fresh red chillies, finely chopped
2 tablespoons sugar
⅓ cup red wine vinegar
¼ cup olive oil

1 Arrange rocket, flowers and radicchio attractively on serving plates. Top with grapefruit and chicken.
2 To make dressing, place pine nuts, bay leaves, chillies, sugar, vinegar and oil in a bowl and whisk to combine. Just prior to serving, drizzle dressing over salad.

Serves 4 • Preparation 10 minutes

Israeli kumquat chicken salad with mixed wild rice

2 lb/1kg lean chicken, diced
1 teaspoon freshly ground black salt
1 teaspoon pepper
1 teaspoon paprika
1 teaspoon ground cumin
1 teaspoon onion powder
2 cups orange juice
¼ cup dry white wine
2 onions, diced
4 tablespoons apricot jam
4 tablespoons peach jam

4 tablespoons honey
2 tablespoons lemon juice
2 tablespoons lime juice
1 lb/500g fresh or canned kumquat
¼ cup wild rice
½ cup brown rice
1 cup white rice
1 bunch basil, leaves thinly sliced
3½ oz/100g toasted, pistachio nuts
  chopped

1 Place the diced chicken in a plastic bag and add the salt, pepper, paprika, ground cumin and onion powder and seal the bag. Shake vigorously to coat the chicken with the spice mix then thread the spiced chicken pieces onto wooden skewers and place them in a shallow baking dish. Set aside.

2 Meanwhile mix the orange juice, wine, onions, both jams, honey, lemon juice, lime juice and kumquats in a saucepan and heat until just about to boil. Pour half this mixture (reserving the remaining mixture) over the chicken skewers and marinate for 2 hours.

3 While the chicken is marinating, prepare the rice. Bring a large pot of salted water to the boil and add the wild rice. Boil for 5 minutes then add the brown rice. Boil these together for a further 10 minutes before adding the white rice and simmering for 15 minutes. Drain thoroughly and keep warm.

4 Heat a grill pan, barbecue or griller and cook the chicken skewers until cooked through, brushing them with the remaining kumquat mixture as they cook.

5 Fold the finely sliced fresh basil and chopped pistachio nuts through the rice then serve with the chicken skewers. Drizzle any remaining kumquat mixture over if desired.

Serves 6–8 • Preparation 2 hours • Cooking 40 minutes

Marsala quail salad

6 quail
1 oz/30g butter
½ cup cream
¾ cup dry Marsala
1 curly endive, leaves separated
1 witlof, leaves separated
1 radicchio, leaves separated
1 bunch watercress
1 pear, peeled, cored and sliced
2 oz/60g pecans

Marsala sauce
½ cup cream
2 tablespoons mayonnaise
2 teaspoons dry Marsala

1 Place quail on a rack in a baking pan and bake for 20 minutes. Cool slightly, then break into serving-size portions.
2 Melt butter in a saucepan. Add cream and Marsala, bring to the boil, then reduce heat and simmer for 5 minutes. Add quail and cook for 5 minutes longer. Set aside to cool.
3 To make sauce, combine cream, mayonnaise and Marsala and beat well to combine.
4 Arrange endive, witlof, radicchio, watercress and pear in a serving bowl. Top with quail, sprinkle with pecans and drizzle sauce over. Serve immediately.

Serves 6 • Preparation 10 minutes • Cooking 30 minutes

Indian salad of spiced chicken and dhal

7½ cups vegetable stock
1½ cups dried lentils
juice of 2 lemons
2 tablespoons vegetable oil
1 tablespoon curry powder
1 tablespoon garam masala
1 teaspoon turmeric
salt and freshly ground black pepper

4 large chicken breast fillets, skin removed
1 small cauliflower, cut into florets
1½ cups fresh or frozen peas
2 small tomatoes, deseeded and diced
1 cucumber, peeled and diced
2 spring onions, sliced
¼ cup fresh mint, chopped
2 large bunches watercress, trimmed

1 Bring 6 cups of vegetable stock to the boil and add the lentils. Simmer until the lentils are tender but still retain their shape, about 20 minutes. Drain well then transfer the lentils to a large bowl and add the lemon juice and 1 tablespoon of the oil. Mix well, cover and chill.

2 Combine the curry powder, garam masala and turmeric in a plastic bag with salt and pepper to taste then add the chicken breasts to the bag. Seal the bag and shake vigorously, allowing the spices to coat the chicken breasts evenly. Heat a grill pan or non-stick frying pan with the remaining oil until smoking then add the chicken breasts to the pan and cook until cooked through and golden brown on both sides, about 5 minutes. Remove the chicken and set aside.

3 To the same pan, add the remaining stock and bring to the boil. Add the cauliflower and peas and cook over high heat until vegetables are crisp-tender and most of liquid has evaporated, about 5 minutes. Add this vegetable mixture to the lentils and mix well. Add the tomatoes, cucumber, spring onions and fresh mint and mix well, adding more salt and pepper to taste.

4 Slice the chicken into diagonal strips then gently mix these into the salad. Arrange the watercress on a platter and top with the salad mixture, arranging so that there is plenty of chicken visible. Garnish with extra mint.

Serves 6–8 • Preparation 15 minutes • Cooking 35 minutes

Tandoori lamb salad with black onion seeds and sesame

12 large lamb cutlets
1 cup sesame seeds
½ cup black onion seeds

Marinade
1 large onion, chopped
1 in/25mm piece fresh ginger, grated
juice of 1 lemon
½ cup plain yoghurt
2 teaspoons ground coriander
2 teaspoons ground cumin
½ teaspoon ground turmeric
¼ teaspoon Cayenne pepper

1 tablespoon garam masala
¼ teaspoon mace
1 teaspoon salt

Salad
8 oz/250g baby spinach leaves
7 oz/200g mixed baby lettuce leaves
4 spring onions, sliced
2 tablespoons white vinegar
3 tablespoons peanut oil
salt and freshly ground black pepper
few drops of toasted sesame oil

1 To make the marinade, place the onion, ginger, lemon juice and 1 tablespoon water in a food processor with the yoghurt, spices and salt and process until the mixture is smooth. Remove from the processor and pour over the lamb cutlets, turning to coat both sides of the lamb. Marinate for a minimum of 4 hours or up to 8 hours.

2 Preheat the oven to 440°F/220°C. When you are ready to cook, mix the sesame seeds and onion seeds together and place them on a plate. Remove the lamb cutlets from the marinade one at a time, allowing the excess to run off, then dip each cutlet in the sesame mixture, coating both sides. Place the coated cutlets on a non-stick baking tray and bake in the preheated oven for 10 minutes for medium rare, or longer if you prefer.

3 Meanwhile, prepare the salad. Wash and dry the spinach and mixed lettuce leaves and place them, with the spring onions, in a large salad bowl. Whisk together the vinegar and peanut oil with salt and pepper to taste then add the few drops of sesame oil, continuing to whisk until the dressing is thick. Toss the salad with the dressing until the leaves are well coated then divide the salad between 6 plates. Arrange 2 cutlets on each plate and serve immediately.

Black onion seeds (nigella) are available from Indian grocery stores. If unavailable, you can use unhulled sesame seeds.

Serves 6 • Preparation 15 minutes plus marinating time • Cooking 10 minutes

Chicken grape salad

5 oz/150g small shell pasta
2 lb/1kg chicken, cooked and cooled
5 oz/150g seedless green grapes, halved
¼ cup fresh tarragon
2 tablespoons mayonnaise
2 tablespoons natural yoghurt
freshly ground black pepper

1 Bring a large saucepan of salted water to the boil, add the pasta and cook for
   8 minutes or until just firm in the centre (al dente). Drain, rinse under cold running
   water, then drain again and set aside to cool completely.
2 Remove skin from chicken and discard. Strip flesh from chicken and chop. Place pasta,
   chicken, grapes and tarragon in a bowl and stir to combine.
3 Place mayonnaise, yoghurt and black pepper in a small bowl and mix to combine.
   Spoon over chicken mixture and toss to coat all ingredients. Serve at room
   temperature.

Serves 4 • Preparation 30 minutes • Cooking 10 minutes

Italian sausage with zucchini and mezuma leaves

2 medium zucchini, cut into 1cm slices
12 oz/350g Italian sausages
1 thin baguette, cut into 2cm slices
2 tablespoons olive oil
2 bunches mezuma leaves
¼ cup basil leaves, shredded
4 oz/125g semi-sun-dried tomatoes
1½ oz/45g Parmesan cheese, grated

Dressing
¼ cup olive oil
2 tablespoons lemon juice
salt and freshly ground black pepper

1 Lightly brush a chargrill pan with oil, and heat. Char-grill zucchini 2–3 minutes each side, then remove and set aside.

2 Add the sausages and cook for 6–8 minutes, turning frequently, then remove from the grill and set aside to cool. When cool, slice sausages into 1 in/25mm slices.

3 Brush slices of bread with the oil, and cook on chargrill for 2–3 minutes each side. Combine mezuma leaves, basil, sausages, zucchini, sun-dried tomatoes and Parmesan in a large bowl.

4 To make the dressing, mix together oil, lemon juice, salt and pepper, and whisk. Drizzle dressing over salad before serving.

Serves 4 • Preparation 25 minutes • Cooking 15 minutes

Thai beef salad

1 lb/500g rump steak
freshly ground black pepper
1 small red chilli, finely chopped
2 tablespoons lime juice
2 tablespoons fish sauce
2 tablespoons grated palm sugar or brown sugar
1 teaspoon sesame oil
¼ Chinese cabbage, finely shredded
1 cup fresh coriander sprigs
1 cup fresh mint sprigs
4 oz/125g snow peas, trimmed
1 Lebanese cucumber, sliced
1 small red onion, thinly sliced
7 oz/200g cherry tomatoes, halved

1 Trim any excess fat and sinew from the steak. Season with black pepper.
2 Cook the steak on a lightly oiled chargrill for a few minutes until medium rare.
   Remove and rest for 10 minutes before slicing across the grain into thin strips.
3 Put the chilli, lime juice, fish sauce, palm sugar and sesame oil in a jug and whisk
   to combine.
4 Combine the cabbage, half the coriander, the mint, snow peas, cucumber, onion
   and tomatoes on a large salad platter or a individual plates.
5 Top with the sliced steak, drizzle with dressing and garnish with the remaining
   coriander.

Serves 4 • Preparation 30 minutes • Cooking 10 minutes

Oregano lamb and couscous salad

1 lb/500g lamb loin
2 cloves garlic, crushed
1 teaspoon ground cinnamon
1 teaspoon ground allspice
2 tablespoons lemon juice
1 teaspoon honey
1 tablespoon olive oil
¼ cup fresh oregano, chopped
1 cup couscous
2 cups chicken stock
14 oz/400g canned chickpeas, rinsed and drained
7 oz/200g cherry tomatoes, halved
2 cups fresh flat-leaf parsley, roughly chopped
1 cup raisins
2 oranges, cut into segments

1 Trim the lamb loin of all excess fat and sinew. Put the garlic, cinnamon, allspice, lemon juice, honey, olive oil and oregano in a jug and whisk to combine. Pour over the lamb, cover and marinate in the refrigerator for 4 hours or overnight.

2 Put the couscous in a bowl. Bring the chicken stock to the boil and pour over the couscous. Allow to stand for 10 minutes or until all the liquid is absorbed.

3 Lightly oil a chargrill or barbecue and cook the marinated lamb loin over a medium-high heat for about 10 minutes or until medium-rare. Allow to stand for 5 minutes before slicing.

4 Fold the lamb, chickpeas, tomatoes, parsley, raisins and oranges through the couscous and serve.

Serves 4 • Preparation 20 minutes plus marinating time • Cooking 15 minutes

Warm Thai chicken salad

3 chicken breasts
2 teaspoons Thai flavour seasoning
1 teaspoon oil
1 red capsicum, deseeded and cut into strips
1 green capsicum, deseeded and cut into strips
1 eggplant, sliced
1 red onion, cut into rings
½ cos lettuce, shredded

Dressing
½ cup olive oil
1¼ cups malt vinegar
1 teaspoon Thai seasoning

1 Flatten the chicken breasts slightly to an even thickness. Mix the Thai seasoning
   and oil together and rub well into the chicken. Cover and stand for 20 minutes before
   cooking.
2 Heat the barbecue to medium-high and oil the hotplate and the grill bars. Place
   the chicken on the grill and cook for 4 minutes on each side. Place the vegetables
   (except the lettuce) on the hotplate, drizzle with a little oil and cook for 5–8 minutes,
   tossing and turning to cook through. Pile lettuce onto individual plates and place the
   barbecued vegetables in the centre. Cut the chicken into thin diagonal slices and
   arrange over and around the vegetables.
3 Mix the dressing ingredients together and pour over the salad. Serve with crusty
   bread.

Serves 3 • Preparation 35 minutes • Cooking 12 minutes

Warm duck and mango salad

8 oz/250g boneless duck breast
2 teaspoons sesame oil
1 ripe mango
4 oz/125g mixed dark salad leaves, such as baby spinach and rocket
4 oz/125g sugar snap peas, chopped
4 spring onions, sliced diagonally

Dressing
3 tablespoons extra virgin olive oil
juice of 1 lime
1 teaspoon clear honey
¼ cup fresh coriander, chopped
freshly ground black pepper

1 Skin the duck breasts and cut into strips. Heat the sesame oil in a wok or large frying pan, add the duck and stir-fry over a high heat for 4–5 minutes until tender.
2 Slice off the 2 fat sides of the mango close to the stone. Cut a criss-cross pattern across the flesh (but not the skin) of each side with a sharp knife. Push the skin inside out to expose the flesh and cut the cubes off. Place in a salad bowl with the salad leaves, sugar snap peas and spring onions, then toss together gently to mix.
3 To make the dressing, whisk together the olive oil, lime juice, honey, coriander and black pepper in a small bowl until thoroughly mixed. Add the warm duck to the mango salad, drizzle over the dressing, then toss together to mix. Garnish with fresh coriander.

Serves 4 • Preparation 25 minutes • Cooking 10 minutes

Chicken and avocado salad

3 skinless chicken breast fillets, cooked and sliced
1 small head lettuce, shredded
1 large red onion, thinly sliced
½ cup olive oil
¼ cup red wine vinegar
salt and freshly ground black pepper
2 avocados, peeled and sliced

1 Place chicken, lettuce and onion in a bowl. Thoroughly combine oil and vinegar and season to taste with salt and pepper. Pour over salad, toss gently, then arrange chicken on a serving plate. Garnish with avocado and reserve.

Serves 6 • Preparation 10 minutes

grains, pulses and pasta

Grains, pulses and pasta can form the basis of many satisfying salad dishes. Combine them with fresh greens or other vegetables and a few herbs and spices and you will have a wonderful balance of flavours, textures and nutrients.

Japanese rice noodle salad

8 oz/250g long, flat rice noodles
1 teaspoon olive oil
1 oz/25cm piece ginger, grated
1–2 small fresh red chillies, deseeded and minced
1 red capsicum, cut into small chunks
6 spring onions, sliced on the diagonal
½ bunch coriander
juice of 1 lime
1 tablespoon Japanese rice vinegar
1 tablespoon soy sauce
2 tablespoons vegetable stock
3 tablespoons sesame seeds

1 Fill a large jug or bowl with hot (not boiling) water and immerse the rice noodles, allowing them to soak until soft, about 5–10 minutes. Drain and rinse under cold water to refresh them, then place the noodles in a large mixing bowl.

2 Heat the olive oil in a small non-stick pan and add the ginger and chillies and sauté gently for 1–2 minutes. Add the chopped capsicum pieces, raise the heat to medium-high and stir-fry until the capsicum pieces are softened. Add the spring onion slices and continue to cook for a further 2 minutes.

3 Tip the capsicum mixture into the mixing bowl with the noodles and add the coriander, tossing thoroughly.

4 In a small jug, whisk together the lime juice, rice vinegar, soy and stock and toss through the noodles. Sprinkle with the sesame seeds and chill before serving.

Serves 2 • Preparation 20 minutes • Cooking 15 minutes

Marinated bean salad

3½ oz/100g green beans, cut in half
2 small zucchini, cut into matchsticks
1 small carrot, cut into matchsticks
8 oz/250g canned red kidney beans, drained and rinsed
8 oz/250g canned chickpeas, drained and rinsed
8 oz/250g canned lima beans, drained and rinsed
1 small red capsicum, cut into strips
¼ cup fresh parsley, chopped
¼ cup fresh basil, chopped

Dressing
¼ cup olive oil
1½ tablespoons red wine vinegar
1 clove garlic, crushed
freshly ground black pepper

1 Steam the green beans, zucchini and carrot until just tender. Drain and refresh under cold running water.
2 To make dressing, place oil, vinegar, garlic and black pepper to taste in a screw-top jar and shake well to combine.
3 Place cooked vegetables, red kidney beans, chickpeas, lima beans, capsicum, parsley and basil in a large salad bowl. Spoon over dressing and toss to combine. Cover and refrigerate for 4–6 hours. Just prior to serving, toss again.

Canned beans are a quick and nutritious alternative to dried beans. There is some loss of B vitamins during canning, but not a lot. A couple of cans of beans in your cupboard are always a handy standby for an easy, no-fuss, high-fibre meal.

Serves 4 • Preparation 4–6 hours • Cooking 15 minutes

Tuna barley niçoise

2 pink potatoes, unpeeled
1 teaspoon olive oil
salt and freshly ground black pepper
2 fresh rosemary sprigs, leaves removed
  and chopped
1 litre mild vegetable stock
1 teaspoon fresh oregano
1 teaspoon fresh marjoram
1 cup pearl barley
1 red onion, sliced into rings
6 tuna steaks, about 180g each
1 lb/500g green beans, blanched

½ cup fresh parsley, chopped
4 oz/120g mixed salad leaves
7 oz/200g roasted capsicum, sliced
2 Roma tomatoes, finely chopped
5 oz/150g Kalamata olives, finely chopped

Dressing
4 cloves garlic, minced
1 teaspoon mixed dried herbs
1–2 tablespoons virgin olive oil
1 teaspoon Dijon mustard
½ cup vegetable stock

1 Preheat oven to 440°F/220°C. Wash the potatoes well and slice (do not peel). Brush
   lightly or spray with olive oil. Sprinkle with salt, pepper and rosemary and bake on an
   oven tray for 45 minutes, turning during the cooking time.

2 Meanwhile, bring the stock to a boil and add the oregano and marjoram. Add the
   barley, cover and simmer for 40 minutes. Remove from heat and set aside. Soak the
   red onion in cold water for 30 minutes, then drain.

3 Season the tuna steaks with salt and pepper and cook on a preheated grill pan for
   2 minutes each side, until just cooked.

4 To make the dressing, whisk together all ingredients until thick, then set aside. Mix
   green beans, onions rings, parsley and half the dressing with the warm barley and
   toss thoroughly to distribute.

5 To assemble, place several slices of potato on the centre of each plate, top with
   6 salad leaves, a generous spoonful of barley mixture, some roasted capsicum and a
   cooked tuna steak. Place teaspoonsful of finely chopped tomato and olives around the
   salad, then drizzle everything with remaining dressing. Sprinkle with extra parsley
   and serve at room temperature.

Serves 6 • Preparation 45 minutes • Cooking 1 hour 30 minutes

South American bean salad

1½ lb/800g cans canellini beans, drained and rinsed
1 small red onion, thinly sliced
1 small red capsicum, roasted and thinly sliced
1 jalapeño chilli, deseeded and diced
3 cups watercress sprigs, washed
¼ cup flat-leaf parsley leaves
2 tablespoons extra virgin olive oil
1 tablespoon lemon juice
2 tablespoons red wine vinegar
½ teaspoon sugar
salt and freshly ground black pepper

1 Place beans in a serving bowl. Add red onion, red capsicum, chilli, watercress and parsley.
2 Combine olive oil, lemon juice, red wine vinegar, sugar, salt and pepper in a small bowl.
3 Pour dressing over and toss to combine.

To roast capsicum, cut into quarters, remove seeds and place under a hot grill for 6–8 minutes or until the skin blackens. Remove skin and thinly slice.

Serves 4 • Preparation 10 minutes • Cooking 8 minutes

Greek orzo salad with olives and capsicums

12 oz/350g orzo or rice-shaped pasta
6 oz/170g feta cheese, crumbled
1 red capsicum, finely chopped
1 yellow capsicum, finely chopped
1 green capsicum, finely chopped
6 oz/170g pitted Kalamata olives, chopped
4 spring onions, sliced
2 tablespoons drained capers
3 tablespoons pine nuts, toasted

Dressing
juice and zest of 2 lemons
1 tablespoon white wine vinegar
4 large cloves garlic, minced
1½ teaspoons dried oregano
1 teaspoon Dijon mustard
1 teaspoon ground cumin
100mL olive oil

1 Cook the orzo in a large pot of boiling salted water until tender but still firm to bite. Drain and rinse with cold water then place in a large bowl with a little olive oil.

2 Add the feta, capsicums, olives, spring onions and capers.

3 To make the dressing, whisk together the lemon juice and zest, vinegar, garlic, oregano, mustard and cumin in a small bowl. Gradually add the olive oil, then season to taste with salt and pepper.

4 Drizzle the dressing over the salad and toss thoroughly. Garnish with the toasted pine nuts and serve.

Serves 4 • Preparation 30 minutes • Cooking 30 minutes

Warm lima bean and prosciutto salad with rocket

1 lb/500g dried lima beans
2 tablespoons olive oil
½ teaspoon dried chilli flakes
3 cloves garlic, minced
3½ oz/100g prosciutto, roughly chopped
salt and freshly ground black pepper
10 basil leaves, torn
2 handfuls rocket leaves

1   Place the lima beans in a large bowl of warm water and soak overnight.

2   The next day, drain the beans and place in a saucepan of cold water. Bring to the boil and simmer for 1 hour or until just tender. Drain, reserving a ladle or two of the cooking water.

3   Heat the olive oil in a medium saucepan. Add the chilli flakes and garlic and sauté briefly until the garlic is golden. Add the prosciutto and stir over moderate heat until beginning to brown, about 2 minutes. Add the lima beans and cook, tossing occasionally, until heated through, about 3 minutes, adding some of the reserved cooking water if the mixture seems a little dry.

4   Season with salt and pepper and add the torn basil leaves and rocket. Toss gently then serve warm.

Serves 4 • Preparation 12 hours • Cooking 1 hour 10 minutes

Pasta salad with roasted garlic

20 unpeeled cloves garlic
8 rashers bacon, chopped
1 oz/30g butter
2 cups breadcrumbs, made from stale bread
½ cup fresh mixed herbs, chopped
freshly ground black pepper
1¼ lb/750g spaghetti

1 Preheat oven to 360°F/180°C. Place unpeeled garlic cloves on a lightly greased baking tray and bake for 10–12 minutes or until soft and golden. Peel garlic and set aside.

2 Cook bacon in a frying pan over a medium heat for 4–5 minutes or until crisp. Drain on absorbent paper.

3 Melt butter in a clean frying pan, add breadcrumbs, herbs and black pepper to taste and cook, stirring for 4–5 minutes or until breadcrumbs are golden.

4 Bring a large saucepan of salted water to the boil, add the pasta and cook for 8 minutes or until just firm in the centre (al dente). Drain well and place in a warm serving bowl. Add garlic, bacon and breadcrumb mixture, toss and serve immediately.

The garlic can be roasted and the bacon and breadcrumb mixture cooked several hours in advance, leaving just the cooking of the pasta and the final assembly of the salad to do at the last minute.

Serves 8 • Preparation 15 minutes • Cooking 40 minutes

Gingered Thai rice salad

2 cups long-grain rice
5 spring onions, finely chopped on the diagonal
3 medium carrots, coarsely grated
4 baby bok choy, washed and chopped
2 kaffir lime leaves, finely sliced
½ cup coriander, coarsely chopped
1½ cups chopped roasted peanuts
1 tablespoon black sesame seeds
2 tablespoons Thai basil, finely chopped

Dressing
2 tablespoons peanut oil
juice of 2 limes
3 tablespoons Thai fish sauce
2 tablespoons palm sugar
2 tablespoons sweet chilli sauce
1 tablespoon minced ginger
pinch of chilli powder or Cayenne pepper
salt and freshly ground black pepper

1   Bring a large pot of salted water to the boil then add the rice and simmer for 8–10 minutes or until tender. Drain and rinse thoroughly in cold water then drain again.

2   Meanwhile, make the dressing. Whisk together the oil, lime juice, fish sauce, palm sugar, sweet chilli sauce, ginger, chilli powder and salt and pepper and allow to sit until the rice is ready.

3   Prepare all the vegetables then mix thoroughly with the lime leaves, coriander, peanuts and sesame seeds. Add the cooked rice and mix well.

4   Toss the rice and vegetable mixture with the dressing, tossing thoroughly to coat all the ingredients, then add the Thai basil and serve.

Serves 6 • Preparation 20 minutes • Cooking 10 minutes

Roasted corn and bean salad Mexicana

4 ears of corn
2 red capsicums, chopped
1 green capsicum, chopped
1 red onion, chopped
1 tablespoon paprika
1 tablespoon ground cumin
2 tablespoons oil
2 cloves garlic, minced
6 yellow baby squash
14 oz/400g canned lima beans, rinsed
14 oz/400g canned red kidney beans, rinsed
½ cup vegetable stock
1 teaspoon Tabasco
1 teaspoon sugar
juice of 2 limes
½ cup fresh coriander, chopped
salt and freshly ground black pepper

1 Cut the corn from the ears and discard the cobs.
2 In a large non-stick pan, combine the onion, capsicum, paprika, cumin and corn and cook over a high heat until the vegetables begin to blacken and blister, stirring often. Remove from the pan and set aside.
3 Add the oil, garlic and squash to the same pan and cook for 4 minutes, stirring constantly.
4 Add the lima beans, kidney beans, stock, Tabasco and sugar and cook until the liquid has evaporated and the vegetables are hot.
5 Remove from the heat and add lime juice, fresh coriander and salt and pepper to taste. Add the corn mixture and toss thoroughly to coat all the vegetables. Serve warm or at room temperature.

Serves 6–8 • Preparation 12 minutes • Cooking 15 minutes

Middle Eastern bean and artichoke salad

20 oz/600g green beans
28 oz/800g canned chickpeas, drained and rinsed
8 marinated artichoke hearts, quartered
1 small red onion, peeled and very finely sliced
1 medium carrot, grated
½ cup parsley, chopped
½ cup coriander, chopped
2 tablespoons fresh dill
2 tablespoons white wine vinegar
3 tablespoons olive oil
1 clove garlic, minced
1 teaspoon mustard
1 teaspoon ground cumin
juice of 1 large lemon
salt and freshly ground black pepper
3½ oz/100g hazelnuts, toasted and roughly chopped

1 Steam the beans until bright green and crisp-tender (do not overcook), drain well and refresh in cold water, then cut diagonally in half.
2 Place in a large bowl and add the chickpeas, artichoke hearts, red onion, carrot, parsley, coriander and dill. Stir to combine thoroughly.
3 In a jug, whisk the vinegar, olive oil, garlic, mustard, cumin, lemon juice and salt and pepper. When emulsified (thick) pour over the vegetable mixture and toss very well to coat the vegetables in the dressing.
4 Sprinkle with toasted hazelnuts and serve.

Serves 6–8 • Preparation 10 minutes • Cooking 12–15 minutes

Indian chickpea salad with spinach

2 cups dried chickpeas
4 onions
1 teaspoon whole cloves
4 bay leaves
¼ cup peanut or olive oil
4 cloves garlic, minced
1 teaspoon ground turmeric

2 teaspoons ground cumin
2 teaspoons garam masala
3 tablespoons tomato paste
2 red capsicums, sliced
4 medium zucchini, sliced on the diagonal
salt and freshly ground black pepper
1 lb/500g baby spinach

1 Pick over the chickpeas and remove any that are discoloured. Place all remaining chickpeas in a large saucepan and cover with cold water. Peel 2 of the onions and chop in half. Place these in the saucepan with the chickpeas. Add the cloves and bay leaves, bring to the boil and simmer for 10 minutes, then remove the chickpeas from the heat, cover and allow to stand for 2 hours. Strain the chickpeas, discarding the onions, cloves and bay leaves, but reserving the soaking water.

2 Meanwhile, chop the remaining 2 onions. Heat the oil and sauté the onions and the minced garlic. Add all the spices and cook briefly to release their fragrance. Add the soaked chickpeas and 2 cups of the soaking water, the tomato paste and the red capsicum strips.

3 Cover and simmer gently for about 20 minutes until the chickpeas soften and the liquid evaporates. Add the zucchini and salt and pepper to taste, stir well then remove from the heat. Allow to cool slightly then fold through the spinach leaves.

4 Cool completely and serve.

Never add salt to pulses until after the initial cooking or soaking because the salt will toughen the skin of the bean and inhibit its ability to absorb liquid.

Serves 8 • Preparation 2 hours • Cooking 30 minutes

Pasta and asparagus salad

1 lb/500g chilli linguine
8 oz/250g asparagus, cut in half
5 oz/150g watercress, broken into sprigs
2 oz/60g butter
4 sprigs fresh rosemary, leaves removed and chopped
freshly ground black pepper
fresh Parmesan cheese shavings
lime wedges

1 Bring a large saucepan of salted water to the boil, add the pasta and cook for
  8 minutes or until just firm in the centre (al dente). Drain well and rinse under cold
  running water, drain again and set aside.
2 Steam the asparagus until tender. Add asparagus and watercress to pasta and toss
  to combine.
3 Place butter and rosemary in a small saucepan and cook over a low heat until
  butter is golden. Divide pasta between serving bowls, then drizzle with rosemary-
  flavoured butter and top with black pepper and Parmesan cheese to taste. Serve
  with lime wedges.

**Chilli pasta is available from delicatessens and specialty food stores. If unavailable,
use ordinary pasta and add some chopped fresh chilli to the butter and rosemary
mixture.**

Serves 4 • Preparation 10 minutes • Cooking 25 minutes

Spicy wild rice salad

14 oz/400g wild rice blend (brown and wild rice mix)
2 tablespoons vegetable oil
2 onions, cut into thin wedges
1 teaspoon ground cumin
½ teaspoon ground cinnamon
¼ teaspoon ground cloves
¼ teaspoon ground ginger
2 carrots, thinly sliced
1 teaspoon honey
2 oranges, segmented
3 oz/90g pistachios, toasted and roughly chopped

3 oz/90g raisins
2 oz/60g flaked almonds, toasted
3 spring onions, sliced
10 sprigs fresh dill, chopped

Dressing
1 teaspoon Dijon mustard
½ cup olive oil
¼ cup orange juice
1 tablespoon red wine vinegar

1 Combine the rice with 3½ cups water in a saucepan. Bring to the boil, reduce heat to low, cover and cook for 15 minutes. Remove pan from heat, allow to stand covered for 10 minutes. Drain well and set aside to cool.

2 Heat oil in a non-stick frying pan over a medium heat, add onions, cumin, cinnamon, cloves and ginger and cook, stirring, for 10 minutes or until onions are soft and slightly caramelised. Add carrots and cook until tender. Stir in honey, then remove from heat and cool slightly.

3 Place rice, carrot mixture, oranges, pistachios, raisins, almonds, spring onions and dill in a bowl and toss to combine.

4 To make dressing, place mustard, oil, orange juice and vinegar in a bowl and whisk to combine. Pour dressing over salad and toss.

If wild-rice blend is unavailable, use ¾ cup brown rice and ¼ cup wild rice. The two varieties of rice can be cooked together.

Serves 4 • Preparation 15 minutes • Cooking 25 minutes

Bulgar wheat salad with grilled capsicums

8 oz/250g bulgar wheat
2 yellow capsicums, quartered and deseeded
250g green beans, halved
2 ripe tomatoes
4 spring onions, sliced
3 oz/90g Brazil nuts, roughly chopped
½ cup fresh parsley, chopped
sea salt and freshly ground black pepper

Dressing
4 tablespoons extra virgin olive oil
1 tablespoon wholegrain mustard
1 clove garlic, crushed
1 teaspoon balsamic vinegar
1 teaspoon white wine vinegar

1   Place the bulgar in a bowl and cover with boiling water to about 2cm above the level of the bulgar and leave to soak for 20 minutes. Meanwhile, preheat the grill to high. Grill the capsicums, skin-side up, for 15–20 minutes until the skin is blistered and blackened all over. Transfer to a plastic bag, seal and leave to cool. When cold enough to handle, remove and discard the charred skins and roughly chop the flesh.

2   Blanch the beans in boiling water for 3–4 minutes, drain, refresh under cold running water and set aside. Put the tomatoes into a bowl, cover with boiling water and leave for 30 seconds. Peel, deseed, then roughly chop the flesh.

3   Combine the ingredients for the dressing and mix well. Drain the bulgar and transfer to a salad bowl. Add the dressing and toss well. Add the vegetables, spring onions, Brazil nuts, parsley and seasoning and toss together gently to mix.

This salad is delicious, filling and extremely nutritious. The mustard and balsamic vinegar in the dressing bring all the other exciting flavours alive.

Serves 4 • Preparation 35 minutes plus soaking time • Cooking 20 minutes

Vietnamese herbed rice noodles with peanuts and asparagus

3 tablespoons rice vinegar
1 tablespoon sugar
1 small red onion, finely sliced
8 oz/250g dried rice noodles
2 bunches asparagus
⅓ cup mint leaves, chopped
⅓ cup coriander leaves, chopped
1 Continental cucumber, peeled, deseeded
  and thinly sliced

6 spring onions, finely sliced
3 Roma tomatoes, finely diced
¾ cup roasted peanuts, lightly crushed
juice of 2 limes
2 teaspoons fish sauce
2 teaspoons olive oil
½ teaspoon chilli flakes

1 First, whisk the vinegar and sugar together and pour over the onion rings. Allow to marinate for 1 hour, tossing frequently.

2 Cover noodles in boiling water and soak for 5 minutes, then drain thoroughly.

3 Cut the tough stalks off the asparagus, and cut the remaining stalks into 2cm lengths. Simmer the asparagus in salted water for 2 minutes until bright green and crisp-tender. Rinse in cold water to refresh.

4 Toss the noodles with the onion and vinegar mixture while the noodles are still warm, then, using kitchen scissors, cut the noodles into manageable lengths.

5 Add the cooked asparagus, mint, coriander, cucumber, spring onions, tomatoes and peanuts and toss thoroughly.

6 Whisk the lime juice, fish sauce, oil and chilli flakes together and drizzle over the noodle salad. Serve at room temperature.

Serves 4 • Preparation 1 hour 10 minutes • Cooking 10 minutes

Bean and artichoke salad

8 oz/250g green beans, cut into 1 in/25mm pieces
1 red capsicum, cut into thin strips
8 oz/250g canned lima or butter beans, drained and rinsed
14 oz/400g marinated artichoke hearts, drained and halved
2 tablespoons olive oil
4 tablespoons vinegar
freshly ground black pepper

1 Steam green beans until just tender. Refresh under cold running water. Set aside.
2 Place capsicum strips in a bowl of iced water for 20 minutes or until curled.
3 Place green beans, capsicum, lima or butter beans, artichoke hearts, oil, vinegar and black pepper in a bowl and toss to combine.

Serves 4 • Preparation 25 minutes • Cooking 5 minutes

Italian tuna and bean salad

6 oz/185g canned tuna in oil
14 oz/400g canned borlotti beans, drained and rinsed
1 small red onion, thinly sliced
2 stalks celery, thinly sliced
½ cup fresh flat-leaf parsley, chopped

Dressing
4 tablespoons olive oil
2 tablespoons balsamic or white wine vinegar
salt and freshly ground black pepper

1 Drain the tuna and reserve the oil. To make the dressing, whisk the reserved tuna oil with the olive oil and vinegar, then season.
2 Flake the tuna into a large bowl and mix with the borlotti beans, red onion, celery and parsley. Spoon over the dressing and toss well to combine.

Serves 4 • Preparation 5 minutes

Insalata spirale

1 lb/500g spiral pasta
3½ oz/100g sun-dried tomatoes, thinly sliced
3½ oz/100g marinated artichoke hearts, chopped
2½ oz/75g sun-dried or roasted capsicum, chopped
4 oz/125g marinated black olives
12 fresh basil leaves
2 oz/60g Parmesan cheese, shaved
1 tablespoon olive oil
3 tablespoons balsamic or red wine vinegar

1 Bring a large saucepan of salted water to the boil, add the pasta and cook for
  8 minutes or until just firm in the centre (al dente). Drain, rinse under cold running
  water and set aside to cool completely.
2 Place pasta, sun-dried tomatoes, artichokes, capsicum, olives, basil, Parmesan, oil
  and vinegar in a bowl and toss to combine. Cover and refrigerate for at least 2 hours
  or overnight.

Serves 4 • Preparation 2 hrs 20 minutes • Cooking 20 minutes

Three bean rice salad

1 cup brown rice
6 oz/175g frozen baby broad beans
14 oz/400g canned black-eye beans, drained and rinsed
8 oz/250g canned red kidney beans, drained and rinsed
1 red capsicum, deseeded and cut into pieces
1 bunch spring onions, chopped

Dressing
5 oz/150mL tomato juice
1 tablespoon olive oil
1 tablespoon white wine vinegar
2 teaspoons Dijon mustard
1 clove garlic, crushed
¼ cup fresh coriander, chopped
freshly ground black pepper

1 Combine the rice with 1½ cups water in a saucepan. Bring to the boil, reduce heat to low, cover and cook for 15 minutes. Remove pan from heat, allow to stand covered for 10 minutes. Meanwhile, cook the baby broad beans in a saucepan of boiling water for 4–5 minutes until tender. Rinse under cold water and drain, then remove the skins if you want. Rinse the rice under cold water, drain and place in a salad bowl.

2 To make the dressing, place the tomato juice, olive oil, vinegar, mustard, garlic, coriander and black pepper in a small bowl and whisk together until thoroughly mixed.

3 Pour the dressing over the rice and stir to mix well. Add the broad beans, black-eyed beans, kidney beans, capsicum and spring onions and mix well. Cover and refrigerate before serving. Garnish with extra coriander.

Serves 4 • Preparation 20 minutes • Cooking 30 minutes

Warm Mediterranean pasta shell salad

6 oz/175g dried pasta shells
5 oz/150g fine green beans, halved
4 spring onions, sliced
1 green capsicum, deseeded and chopped
4 oz/125g cherry tomatoes, halved
1 large ripe avocado, chopped
freshly ground black pepper
2 sprigs fresh basil leaves, torn

Dressing
3 tablespoons olive or sunflower oil
1 tablespoon white wine vinegar
1 tablespoon clear honey
1 teaspoon Dijon mustard

1 To make the dressing, place the oil, vinegar, honey and mustard in a screw-top jar and shake well to combine.

2 Bring a large saucepan of salted water to the boil, add the pasta and cook for 6 minutes. Add the green beans and cook for 2 minutes or until the pasta is tender but still firm to the bite (al dente) and the beans have softened. Drain well.

3 Place the pasta and beans in a large bowl with the spring onions, green capsicum, cherry tomatoes, avocado and seasoning. Add the dressing and toss well. Garnish with the basil.

Serves 4 • Preparation 20 minutes • Cooking 10 minutes

Summer tabouli

6 oz/175g bulgar wheat
2 medium eggs
1 red onion, finely chopped
2 cloves garlic, finely chopped
1 red capsicum, deseeded and finely chopped
1 yellow capsicum, deseeded and finely chopped
¼ cup fresh parsley, chopped
¼ cup fresh coriander, chopped
¼ small bunch chives, chopped
½ cup fresh mint, chopped
grated zest and juice of 1 lemon
grated zest and juice of 1 lime
3 tablespoons olive oil
salt and freshly ground black pepper

1 Place the bulgar in a bowl and cover with boiling water to about 1 in/25mm above the level of the bulgar and leave to soak for 20 minutes, then drain.

2 Meanwhile, bring a saucepan of water to the boil. Add the eggs and boil for 10 minutes. Cool under cold running water, then remove the shells and mash the eggs.

3 Add the onion, garlic, capsicum, parsley, coriander, chives, mint, lemon and lime zest and juice, and the oil to the bulgar wheat, then mix well. Season to taste before serving.

Serves 4 • Preparation 25 minutes • Cooking 10 minutes

Barley, feta and pear salad

1 cup pearl barley
½ cup walnuts
1 cup fresh flat-leaf parsley leaves
3 stalks celery
1–2 firm ripe pears
3½ oz/100g fresh rocket leaves
3½ oz/100g crumbled feta
juice of 1 lemon
3 tablespoons extra virgin olive oil
salt and freshly ground black pepper

1 Place the barley in a large saucepan, partially cover with hot water and boil until tender, about 30 minutes.
2 While barley is cooking, toast walnuts in a small frying pan until golden and fragrant. Set aside.
3 Chop the parsley and cut celery into fine slices. Peel and core pear and cut into fine wedges then mix with the rocket, parsley and celery.
4 Drain barley in a sieve and transfer to a bowl. Add feta and nuts and mix well. Add the rocket mixture.
5 Whisk the lemon juice, oil, salt and pepper then toss through salad until combined.

Serves 6 • Preparation 20 minutes • Cooking 30 minutes

vegetable salads

Vegetables, either hot or cold, and with their great range of colours will suite the eye and delight the palate. Try Asian Gingered Coleslaw with roast chicken or Warm Herbed Potato Salad with roast lamb. Or if you wish go totally vegetarian with Asparagus and Tomato Salad with Cucumber, the possibilities are endless.

Asparagus and baby green beans with hazelnut dressing

6 bunches asparagus, trimmed
2 lb/1kg baby green beans, topped and tailed
2 red capsicums, finely julienned

Dressing
1½ oz/50mL lemon juice
1½ oz/50mL white wine vinegar
3 egg yolks
1 cup hazelnut oil
½ small bunch dill, chopped
1 cup chopped toasted hazelnuts
salt and freshly ground black pepper

1 To make the dressing, combine the lemon juice, vinegar and egg yolks in a food processor and blend until pale and creamy. Slowly drizzle in the oil until the dressing comes together. Stir in the chopped dill and toasted nuts and season to taste.
2 Bring a large saucepan of water to the boil, add the asparagus and beans and simmer for approximately 1–2 minutes until the vegetables are just tender.
3 Drain and toss with the dressing and finely sliced capsicum and serve.

Serves 8–10 as an entrée • Preparation 20 minutes • Cooking 2 minutes

Calabrian salad

4 large potatoes, scrubbed and washed, not peeled
8 firm Roma tomatoes
3 red onions, sliced thinly then soaked in cold water for 30 minutes
15 fresh basil leaves
1 heaped teaspoon dried oregano
4 tablespoons olive oil
3 tablespoons white or red wine vinegar
salt and freshly ground black pepper

1 Cover the potatoes in cold water and boil until just tender all the way through, about 15–20 minutes. Drain and leave aside until just cool enough to handle, then peel and slice thinly.
2 Cut the tomatoes in half and remove the hard inner core. Slice the tomatoes and add them to the potatoes. Add the finely sliced red onion and toss well.
3 Add the basil leaves, oregano, olive oil, vinegar and salt and pepper to taste. Toss everything carefully and serve at once.

Serves 6 • Preparation 1 hour 15 minutes • Cooking 20 minutes

Tuscan panzanella with roasted tomato vinaigrette

10 oz/300g stale, rustic Italian-style bread
2 tablespoons olive oil
2 sprigs fresh rosemary, leaves
  removed and chopped
1 lb/500g assorted tomatoes
1 cucumber
10 Kalamata olives
1 small red onion, finely chopped
10 basil leaves, torn
2 mint leaves, finely sliced
8 sprigs fresh marjoram, leaves
removed and stalks discarded

Dressing
2 small tomatoes
¼ cup olive oil
1 tablespoon red wine vinegar
½ tablespoon balsamic vinegar
2 cloves garlic
salt and freshly ground black pepper

1 Preheat oven to 400°F/200°C. Cut the bread into cubes and toss with olive oil and rosemary. Spread out on a baking tray and bake for 5 minutes until golden, then cool.

2 To make the dressing, heat a heavy pan and brush the skins of the small tomatoes with a little olive oil. Cook these whole tomatoes in the pan until well blackened all over. Purée with the remaining olive oil, vinegars, garlic and salt and pepper to taste. Set aside.

3 Remove the seeds from the other tomatoes and chop the flesh into small chunks. Peel the cucumber and remove the seeds by running a teaspoon along the central seed area. Slice finely. Remove the stones from the olives by squashing them with the wide blade of a knife.

4 In a mixing bowl, place the bread cubes, tomatoes, cucumber, onion, olives and basil leaves. Add the chopped mint and marjoram. Mix well. Pour the dressing over and toss thoroughly. Allow to sit for 10 minutes then serve.

Serves 4 • Preparation 35 minutes • Cooking 10 minutes

Warm salad of capsicum and rosemary

6 large capsicums of assorted colours
2 tablespoons virgin olive oil
1 large red onion, cut into eighths
6 sprigs fresh rosemary
3 cloves garlic, minced
1 tablespoon balsamic vinegar
salt and freshly ground black pepper

1 Slice the 4 sides off each capsicum and discard the seed core. Slice the capsicum pieces into long, thin strips.

2 Heat the olive oil in a frying pan, add the onion and rosemary and sauté on a high heat for 3 minutes. Add the garlic and all the capsicum pieces and toss thoroughly with the rosemary-flavoured oil.

3 Continue cooking over a low heat for 30 minutes, stirring often, until the capsicum pieces are wilted and the onion has caramelised a little. Add the balsamic vinegar and cook for a further 5 minutes.

4 Add salt and pepper to taste and serve warm.

To turn this salad into a true antipasto, cook the capsicum mixture over a medium–high heat (instead of low heat) for 30 minutes until the capsicum pieces are almost meltingly soft.

Serves 4 • Preparation 10 minutes • Cooking 40 minutes

Summer greens with lime and coriander

8 oz/250g snowpeas, topped and tailed
2 bunches asparagus, cut in half
8 oz/250g sugar snap peas, topped and tailed
8 oz/250g shelled fresh peas
4 oz/125g cherry tomatoes, cut in half

Dressing
2 tablespoons lime juice
½ cup coriander, chopped
½ cup olive oil
1 tablespoon white wine vinegar

1 Blanch the snowpeas, asparagus and sugar snap peas in boiling water for 30 seconds, drain and refresh in a bowl of iced cold water. Drain well.

2 Cook peas in boiling water for 2 minutes or until tender, drain and refresh in iced water. Drain well. Combine all green vegetables and cherry tomatoes.

3 For the dressing, whisk the lime juice, coriander, oil and vinegar until well combined, toss over vegetables and serve.

Serves 4–6 • Preparation 15 minutes • Cooking 8 minutes

Warm herbed potato salad

3 lb/1⅓kg russet or Idaho potatoes
2 tablespoons olive oil
4 white onions, sliced
¼ cup fresh dill, chopped
¼ cup fresh chervil, chopped
¼ cup fresh parsley, chopped
zest of 1 lemon
salt and freshly ground pepper

Dressing
⅔ cup olive oil
⅓ cup white wine vinegar
juice of 1 lemon
3 cloves garlic

1 Cut the unpeeled and well washed potatoes into large chunks and boil in salted water for 10 minutes or until tender but not soft. In a separate pan, heat the oil and sauté the onions over a high heat until golden, about 8 minutes. Reduce the heat, cover and cook slowly for 20 minutes.

2 Drain the potatoes and return to the saucepan.

3 In a jug, whisk the dressing ingredients until thickened. Pour the dressing over the hot potatoes and toss, adding the fresh herbs and lemon zest with salt and lots of pepper to taste.

4 Add the caramelised onions and toss thoroughly.

Serves 6–8 • Preparation 20 minutes • Cooking 40 minutes

Mushroom and snowpea salad

8 oz/250g fresh mushrooms
4 oz/125g snowpeas
½ cup mayonnaise
1 tablespoon lime or lemon juice
5 tablespoons light sour cream
¼ cup fresh parsley, chopped
¼ cup chervil, chopped
¼ small bunch chives, chopped
salt and freshly ground black pepper

1 Slice the mushrooms very finely. String the snowpeas, drop into boiling water for about 10 seconds, drain and refresh in cold water. Cut each one into 3 diagonal pieces. Place in a bowl with the mushrooms.
2 In another bowl, combine the mayonnaise with the lime or lemon juice, sour cream, herbs, salt and pepper.
3 Fold the dressing into the mushrooms and snowpeas. Turn into a serving bowl and garnish with the chives.

Serves 4 • Preparation 5 minutes • Cooking 1 minute

Asparagus and tomato salad with cucumber

1 large bunch asparagus
4 small ripe tomatoes
selection of salad greens

Dressing
1 small cucumber
1 tiny spring onion
pinch of salt
freshly ground black pepper
2 tablespoons lemon juice
1 tablespoon sour cream
⅓ cup salad oil
⅓ cup hazelnut or virgin olive oil
⅓ cup dill, chopped

1 First prepare the dressing. Peel the cucumber lightly and remove the seeds. Cut the cucumber into chunks, roughly chop the spring onion and sprinkle them both with salt. Leave to drain for 1 hour in a colander. Rinse in cold water and drain again thoroughly. Purée in a blender or food processor, add the salt, pepper, lemon juice, sour cream and lastly the oils, and purée until a smooth dressing is formed. Add the dill and refrigerate.

2 Prepare and steam the asparagus and cut into 4cm pieces. Peel the tomatoes, halve them and remove the seeds. Cut each half into strips.

3 Arrange the salad greens on serving plates. Toss the asparagus and tomato in the dressing and arrange on each plate on top of the salad greens.

Serves 4 • Preparation 1 hour 10 minutes

Celery, carrot and apple salad with tahini

3 carrots, grated
1 celery heart, thinly sliced
2 apples, peeled, cored and thinly sliced

Dressing
3 tablespoons lemon juice
1 clove garlic, crushed
2 tablespoons tahini
pinch of salt

1 To make the dressing, place the lemon juice, garlic, tahini and 3 tablespoons water in a food processor and blend until smooth. Alternatively, combine with a fork. Season to taste.
2 Toss together the carrots, celery heart and apples and transfer to individual serving bowls. Drizzle with dressing.

Serves 4 • Preparation 15 minutes

Warm vegetable salad with prosciutto

2 leeks, white parts only, sliced
7 oz/200g shelled broad beans or garden peas
5 oz/150g snowpeas
3 tablespoons olive oil
1 clove garlic, thinly sliced
3 spring onions, cut into 5cm lengths
2½ oz/75g baby spinach
salt and freshly ground black pepper
3 slices prosciutto, cut into strips
2 large mushrooms, very thinly sliced
1 tablespoon lemon juice
2 oz/60g Parmesan cheese, shaved

1 Bring a large saucepan of lightly salted water to the boil. Add the leeks and broad beans or peas and cook for 2 minutes, then add the snowpeas and stir for a few seconds. Drain and set aside.

2 Add 2 tablespoons of the oil to the pan, then add the garlic and spring onions. Stir for a minute to soften slightly, then tip in the spinach and stir until it starts to wilt. Add the cooked vegetables to the pan with the remaining oil. Lightly season and fry for 2 minutes to heat through.

3 Add the prosciutto to the pan and heat through for 1–2 minutes. Arrange the mixture on a serving plate. Scatter over the mushrooms and sprinkle with lemon juice. Top with Parmesan, and season with black pepper.

Serves 4 • Preparation 20 minutes • Cooking 10 minutes

Insalata caprese

14 oz/400g Roma tomatoes, thickly sliced
8 oz/250g bocconcini, sliced
½ cup fresh basil leaves, shredded
4 tablespoons extra virgin olive oil
2 tablespoons balsamic vinegar
salt and freshly ground black pepper

1 Arrange tomatoes, bocconcini and basil leaves on individual plates.
2 Drizzle with olive oil and balsamic vinegar, and sprinkle with sea salt and freshly ground black pepper.
3 Serve with crusty bread.

Serves 4 • Preparation 5 minutes

Pila di melanzana

¼ cup olive oil
2 large eggplants
1 red capsicum, quartered
4 Roma tomatoes, sliced
freshly ground black pepper
4 bocconcini, sliced
¼ cup basil leaves
pinch of sea salt

Balsamic dressing
¼ cup olive oil
2 tablespoons balsamic vinegar

1 Preheat the oven to 300°F/150°C.
2 Heat a chargrill pan and brush lightly with oil. Slice each of the eggplants into 8 slices about 10–15mm thick, brush with oil and char-grill 2–3 minutes each side. Place capsicum under a hot grill and cook until skin is black. Remove skin and discard, then finely slice capsicum flesh.
3 Brush tomato slices with oil, sprinkle with pepper, place on a lightly oiled baking tray and roast for 15 minutes. Add the eggplant pieces and cook for a further 10 minutes.
4 On a serving plate, place 2 slices of eggplant, top with 3 strips of capsicum, 3 slices of tomato, 3 slices of bocconcini and 2 more strips of capsicum. Garnish with basil leaves.
5 Combine the dressing ingredients. Drizzle balsamic dressing over dish and top with a good grind of sea salt and black pepper just before serving. Serve with crusty Italian bread.

Serves 4 • Preparation 20 minutes • Cooking 20 minutes

Artichokes la polita

4 globe artichoke hearts
⅓ cup olive oil
6 French shallots, chopped
½ bunch fresh dill, chopped
8 pickling onions, peeled
12 oz/340g baby carrots, peeled
8 small new potatoes
juice of 1 lemon
salt and freshly ground black pepper
2 tablespoons arrowroot

1 Strip away outer leaves of artichokes and trim around base. Cut off top third, scoop out the centre and cut in half. Place in a bowl of cold water with a squeeze of lemon juice to prevent discolouring.

2 Heat half the oil in a large saucepan. Add shallots and dill, sauté until soft.

3 Cross-cut root end of onions and place in saucepan, then add carrots and potatoes. Add lemon juice, remaining oil, salt and pepper and enough water to cover, then cook for 15 minutes.

4 Place artichoke hearts over vegetables and cook for 15 minutes more until tender.

5 With a slotted spoon, remove vegetables to a heated platter and keep warm.

6 Add salt and pepper to the cooking liquid. Blend the arrowroot with enough cold water to make a paste, add to the cooking liquid and stir over heat to thicken sauce. Spoon over vegetables. Serve hot with crusty bread as a main course.

Serves 4 • Preparation 30 minutes • Cooking 40 minutes

Roasted beetroot, orange and fennel salad

3 large beetroots
2 teaspoons brown sugar
1 teaspoon salt
2 sprigs fresh rosemary, leaves removed and chopped
2 tablespoons olive oil
1 bulb fennel
2 blood oranges
3½ oz/100g toasted hazelnuts, crushed

Dressing
½ bunch dill, chopped
2 tablespoons balsamic vinegar
½ cup olive oil
salt and freshly ground black pepper

1 Preheat the oven to 360°F/180°C. Wash and trim the beetroots at root and stem ends but do not peel.
2 In a small bowl, mix together the brown sugar, salt, rosemary and oil until well blended then add the whole beetroots and toss in the oil mixture, making sure that the beetroot skins are all shiny. Wrap each beetroot in foil, place in a baking dish, then roast for approximately 1 hour or until just tender. Peel the beetroots and cut into thick slices.
3 Very finely slice the fennel bulb and peel the oranges, trimming any pith. Cut the orange into segments.
4 To make the dressing, combine the dill, balsamic vinegar, olive oil, salt and pepper and whisk until thick.
5 Arrange the beetroots on a serving platter with the fennel and orange. Drizzle over the dressing then scatter the crushed hazelnuts on top.

Serves 4 • Preparation 30 minutes • Cooking 1 hour

Marinated mushrooms on a bed of leaves

12 oz/350g mixed mushrooms, such as shiitake, large open,
  button and oyster, thickly sliced
3½ oz/100g baby spinach leaves
1 oz/30g watercress, thick stems discarded
4 sprigs fresh thyme

Dressing
3 tablespoons extra virgin olive oil
2 tablespoons unsweetened apple juice
2 teaspoons tarragon white wine vinegar
2 teaspoons Dijon mustard
1 clove garlic, crushed
¼ cup mixed chopped fresh herbs, such as from oregano, thyme,
  chives, basil and parsley
freshly ground black pepper

1 To make the dressing, place the oil, apple juice, vinegar, mustard, garlic, herbs and
   black pepper in a bowl and whisk with a fork to mix thoroughly.
2 Pour the dressing over the mushrooms and stir well. Cover and place in the
   refrigerator for 2 hours.
3 Arrange the spinach and watercress on serving plates. Spoon the mushrooms and
   a little of the dressing over the top and toss lightly to mix. Garnish with fresh thyme.

Serves 4 • Preparation 2 hours 20 minutes

Tomato and onion salad with feta dressing

4 large tomatoes, thinly sliced
1 red onion, thinly sliced
salt and freshly ground black pepper
¼ cup fresh basil, chopped

Dressing
2½ oz/75g feta, crumbled
3 tablespoons natural yoghurt
2 tablespoons extra virgin olive oil
1 tablespoon white wine vinegar

1 Arrange the tomato and onion slices on a large serving plate and season with
   salt and pepper.
2 In a food processor or using a hand blender, blend the feta, yoghurt, oil and vinegar
   until smooth. Drizzle the dressing over the tomatoes, then sprinkle with basil.

Serves 6 • Preparation 5 minutes

Lettuce, avocado and peanut salad

2 small lettuces, leaves separated
1 head chicory, leaves separated
2 small ripe avocados, cut into chunks
3 spring onions, chopped
3 tablespoons salted peanuts

Dressing
1 tablespoon lemon juice
1 clove garlic, crushed
3 tablespoons olive oil
2 tablespoons smooth peanut butter
salt and freshly ground black pepper

1 To make the dressing, put the lemon juice, garlic, oil and peanut butter into a bowl,
   combine thoroughly and season.
2 Arrange the lettuce leaves, chicory and avocado in a large shallow dish. Pour over
   the dressing and sprinkle with spring onions and peanuts.

Serves 4 • Preparation 7 minutes

Roasted vegetable salad

3 red onions, quartered
3 potatoes, scrubbed and cut into wedges
2 zucchini, thickly sliced
2 yellow capsicums, deseeded and thickly sliced
4 tomatoes, halved
2 tablespoons olive oil
sea salt and freshly ground black pepper
Parmesan shavings

Dressing
3 tablespoons extra virgin olive oil
2 tablespoons clear honey
1 tablespoon balsamic vinegar
juice and finely grated zest of ½ lemon

1 Preheat the oven to 400°F/200°C. Place all the vegetables in a shallow roasting tin, drizzle over the olive oil and season. Shake the tray gently to ensure the vegetables are well coated with the oil and seasoning. Bake for about 35 minutes, until the vegetables are really tender and slightly charred at the edges.

2 Meanwhile, mix all the dressing ingredients together. When the vegetables are cooked, pour over the dressing. Toss the salad well and divide between four plates, then top with the Parmesan shavings.

Serves 4 • Preparation 20 minutes • Cooking 35 minutes

Sicilian cauliflower salad

1 small cauliflower
1 oz/30g seedless raisins
1 tablespoon toasted flaked almonds
grated zest of 1 small lemon
¼ cup fresh flat-leaf parsley, chopped

Dressing
juice of 1 small lemon
½ teaspoon ground cinnamon
pinch of Cayenne pepper
5 tablespoons extra virgin olive oil
2 teaspoons balsamic vinegar
1 teaspoon caster sugar
salt and freshly ground black pepper

1 Cut the cauliflower into small florets and slice the stalk into bite-size pieces. Cook in lightly salted boiling water for 2–3 minutes until softened but still firm to the bite. Drain well.
2 To make the dressing, place the lemon juice in a screw-top jar with the cinnamon, Cayenne, oil, vinegar, sugar and seasoning and shake well, or place the ingredients in a bowl and mix with a fork. Pour the dressing over the cauliflower and toss to coat. Leave to cool for 1 hour.
3 Meanwhile, pour enough boiling water over the raisins to cover, then leave for 10 minutes to plump up. Drain and chop roughly. Scatter over the cauliflower with the almonds, lemon zest and parsley and toss lightly.

Serves 4 • Preparation 1 hour 30 minutes • Cooking 10 minutes

Warm spinach salad with walnuts

2 tablespoons walnut oil
5 sun-dried tomatoes in oil, drained and chopped
8 oz/250g baby spinach
1 red onion, sliced into thin rings
2 tablespoons walnut pieces
pinch of salt
¼ cup fresh coriander, chopped

1 Heat the oil in a wok or large heavy-based frying pan. Add the tomatoes, spinach, onion, walnut pieces and salt to taste. Cook for 1 minute or until the spinach begins to wilt, tossing to combine.
2 Transfer the vegetables to a large salad bowl and sprinkle with the coriander to garnish. Serve immediately.

Serves 4 • Preparation 15 minutes • Cooking 1 minutes

Pakistani green bean salad with coriander and ginger

1½ lb/750g fresh snake beans
1 in/25mm piece fresh ginger
1 tablespoon vegetable oil
1 tablespoon sesame oil
1 teaspoon mustard seeds
2 teaspoons ground cumin
½ teaspoon ground turmeric
1 fresh green chilli, finely minced
5 oz/150mL chicken or vegetable stock
juice of 2 lemons
1 bunch fresh coriander, washed, dried then chopped
pinch of salt
3 oz/90g peanuts, roasted and chopped

1 Trim the beans to lengths of 3 in/8cm and discard any discoloured ends. Peel the ginger and cut into fine matchsticks.

2 Heat a wok with the vegetable and sesame oils and, when hot, add the mustard seeds. Allow them to cook for a moment or two until they start popping. Add the ginger and cook for a further minute. Add the ground cumin, turmeric and chilli and stir until fragrant, about 2 minutes.

3 Add all the beans and toss in the flavoured oil to coat them thoroughly. Add the stock, cover and simmer for 5–8 minutes or until the liquid has almost evaporated completely and the beans are tender.

4 Remove the lid and add the lemon juice, coriander and salt to taste. Stir thoroughly to combine all the ingredients then cool. Serve garnished with roasted chopped peanuts and, if desired, lemon wedges.

Serves 4–6 • Preparation 10 minutes • Cooking 15 minutes

Sweet potato and peanut salad

4 lb/1¾kg sweet potato, peeled
6 tablespoons olive oil
20 cloves garlic, unpeeled
salt and freshly ground black pepper
1 red onion, ground
1–2 small red chillies, ground
½ cup fresh herbs such as coriander, parsley, dill, chives or a mixture
2 tablespoons balsamic vinegar
2 cups roasted peanuts

1 Preheat oven to 440°F/220°C. Cut the sweet potato into large chunks. Toss with
   2 tablespoons of the oil and place in a large baking dish with the garlic. Season
   with salt and pepper and bake for about 1 hour or until the sweet potato is tender
   and golden around the edges. Remove from the oven and keep warm.
2 Mix the onion and chilli with the fresh herbs and combine with the sweet potato.
   Whisk the remaining olive oil with the vinegar and toss with the sweet potato
   mixture. Add the peanuts, toss again and serve. Garnished with extra herb sprigs.

Serves 8 as a side dish • Preparation 40 minutes • Cooking 1 hour

Baby spinach, toasted pine nut and avocado salad

3 oz/90g capacollo, sliced
7 oz/200g baby spinach
2 oz/60g pine nuts, toasted
1 avocado, sliced
¼ cup olive oil
2 tablespoons balsamic vinegar
2 oz/60g pecorino cheese, shaved
pinch of sea salt
freshly ground black pepper

1 Place the capacollo under a hot grill and cook until crispy. Place spinach, capacollo, pine nuts and avocado in a bowl.

2 Mix together the oil and balsamic vinegar, pour over the salad, and then toss through the pecorino shavings.

3 Season with salt and pepper and serve.

Capacollo is an Italian cold cut from pork shoulder or nexk. Available from your Italian deli.

Serves 4 • Preparation 10 minutes • Cooking 5 minutes

American potato salad

2 lb/900g new potatoes
⅓ cup dry white wine
½ cup vinaigrette dressing
1 red onion, sliced into rings
1 stalk celery, sliced
2 dill pickles or gherkins, thinly sliced
1 teaspoon capers
4 hard-boiled eggs, peeled and sliced
¼ cup parsley, chopped
salt and freshly ground black pepper

1 Scrub and boil the potatoes in salted water until tender. Peel and slice them while still hot and place into a bowl. Sprinkle with wine, turning the potato slices carefully. Next, sprinkle with the vinaigrette dressing and add the remaining ingredients. Season with salt and pepper to serve.

To vary the recipe fold in ½ cup of mayonnaise or ¼ cup each sour cream and mayonnaise after adding the dressing and before adding the remaining ingredients.

Serves 4 • Preparation 20 minutes • Cooking 20 minutes

Zucchini and hazelnut salad

1½ lb/700g small zucchini
2 tablespoons sunflower oil
5 tablespoons walnut oil
1 tablespoon white wine vinegar
salt and freshly ground black pepper
4 oz/125g whole blanched hazelnuts
6 oz/170g watercress, thick stalks removed
3 oz/90g feta, crumbled

1 Pare the zucchini lengthwise into slivers using a vegetable peeler. In a bowl, mix together the oils and vinegar and season. Add half the zucchini slivers to the mixture, toss lightly and set aside.

2 Brush a large frying pan with a little extra sunflower oil and heat. Lay the remaining zucchini slivers in the pan and cook for 2 minutes on each side or until lightly charred. Remove, season and set aside. Wipe the pan clean.

3 Roughly crush the hazelnuts using a mortar and pestle, or put them in a plastic bag, seal and crush with a rolling pin. Place in the frying pan and fry for 1–2 minutes, until golden.

4 Divide the watercress between serving plates. Spoon some of the marinated zucchini into the centre, reserving some of the marinade. Scatter over the feta and half the toasted hazelnuts. Arrange the charred zucchinis on top, and sprinkle with the rest of the hazelnuts and the reserved marinade.

Serves 6 • Preparation 15 minutes • Cooking 5 minutes

Asian gingered coleslaw

½ large curly cabbage, very finely sliced, about 5 cups
4 baby bok choy, leaves separated and sliced
8 spring onions, julienned
7 oz/200g canned sliced water chestnuts, drained
2 medium carrots, finely julienned
2 stalks lemongrass, finely sliced
4 kaffir lime leaves, finely sliced

Dressing
2 tablespoons mayonnaise
2 tablespoons natural yoghurt
juice of 2 lemons
juice of 1 lime
2 in/5cm piece ginger, grated
4 tablespoons rice vinegar
salt and freshly ground black pepper

Garnish
1 bunch coriander, roughly chopped
½ cup toasted peanuts or sunflower seeds

1 Finely slice the cabbage and mix in a large bowl with the sliced bok choy, spring onions, water chestnuts, carrots and finely sliced lemongrass and lime leaves. Toss thoroughly.

2 In a jug, whisk together all the dressing ingredients until smooth and well seasoned then pour over the salad ingredients and toss thoroughly until all the vegetables are coated with the dressing.

3 To serve, mix through the coriander at the last minute and sprinkle with the peanuts or sunflower seeds.

Serves 6 • Preparation 30 minutes

Tomato and bread salad with pesto dressing

1 baguette, cut into cubes
2 tablespoons olive oil
3 large tomatoes, cut into 1 in/25mm chunks
1 small red onion, thinly sliced
3½ oz/100g feta, crumbled
handful of fresh basil leaves, torn

Dressing
3 tablespoons olive oil
1 red chilli, deseeded and finely chopped
2 tablespoons red pesto
2 tablespoons red wine vinegar
salt and freshly ground black pepper

1 Preheat the grill to high. Toss the bread in the oil to coat evenly and spread out on a baking sheet. Grill for 1–2 minutes until golden, turning occasionally, then leave to cool for 10 minutes.
2 Meanwhile, make the dressing. Heat the oil in a small saucepan and fry the chilli, stirring, for 1 minute or until softened but not browned. Remove from the heat, leave to cool slightly, then add the pesto and vinegar. Whisk with a fork and season.
3 Mix the toasted bread with the tomatoes, onion, and feta. Scatter the basil over the salad. Spoon over the dressing and toss lightly to combine.

Serves 4 • Preparation 25 minutes • Cooking 4 minutes

mixed
salads

A sensational side salad can add flavour and variety to an otherwise simple meal. Many of these easy side salads can also double as light meals. What more delicious meal could there be than Grilled Brie with Beet Salad' served with crusty bread and a nice cool glass of your favourite white wine.

Watercress and pear salad

2 bunches watercress, picked and washed
shavings Parmesan
3 tablespoons olive oil
1 tablespoon lemon juice
½ tablespoon white wine vinegar
salt and freshly ground black pepper
3 beurre bosc pears, finely sliced

1 Wash and dry the watercress well. Slice pears finely and combine with watercress in a bowl.
2 Whisk the olive oil, lemon juice and white wine vinegar with salt and pepper until the mixture has thickened slightly.
3 Drizzle over just enough dressing to coat the leaves. Place on a platter and top with shavings of Parmesan.

Serves 6–8 • Preparation 15 minutes

Warm tomato gratin salad

1 oz/30g butter, melted
4 tablespoons olive oil
2 cups fresh breadcrumbs
½ cup parsley, chopped
20 large basil leaves, finely sliced
½ bunch chives, chopped
salt and freshly ground black pepper
6–8 large tomatoes
7 oz/200g assorted mixed lettuce leaves
1 tablespoon balsamic vinegar

1 Preheat oven to 360°F/180°C. Heat the butter and half the olive oil in a large frying pan and add the breadcrumbs, parsley, basil and chives and toss until golden. Add salt and pepper to taste.

2 Thickly slice the tomatoes and place them on a non-stick oven tray, adding salt and pepper to taste, then press the crumb mixture over the tomatoes to cover each slice.

3 Bake the tomatoes for 10 minutes, then grill just to toast the crumbs.

4 Meanwhile, toss the lettuce leaves with the combined remaining olive oil and vinegar and add salt and pepper to taste.

5 Arrange the lettuce leaves on a platter then top with the tomato slices, allowing each to overlap the previous one. Grind freshly black pepper over and serve.

Serves 4 • Preparation 15 minutes • Cooking 15 minutes

Greek salad

2 Lebanese cucumbers, sliced
4 Roma tomatoes, quartered
2 red onions, quartered
2½ oz/75g feta, crumbled
½ cup whole Kalamata olives, left whole
3 tablespoons extra virgin olive oil
2 tablespoons brown vinegar
pinch of sea salt
freshly ground black pepper
¼ cup oregano leaves

1 Place the cucumber, tomatoes, onion, feta and olives in a bowl.
2 Combine olive oil and vinegar in a separate bowl, and whisk. Pour over the salad, then season with salt and pepper.
3 Garnish with oregano leaves. Serve salad on its own, or with fresh bread.

Serves 4 • Preparation 10 minutes

Witlof salad with apples, blue cheese and pecans

5 heads witlof (Belgian endive)
1 red delicious apple
1 Granny Smith apple
1 tablespoon lemon juice
7 oz/200g young rocket leaves
1 cup coarsely chopped pecans, toasted
3½ oz/100g crumbled blue cheese, such as Gorgonzola or blue castello
¼ cup olive oil
¼ cup walnut oil
¼ cup sherry wine vinegar
1 large French shallot, minced
salt and freshly ground black pepper

1 Cut the witlof in half lengthwise then lay the cut-side down on a board and cut the leaves into thin strips.

2 Thinly slice the unpeeled apples and toss with the lemon juice.

3 Wash the rocket leaves and drain well.

4 Combine witlof strips, apple slices, rocket, toasted pecans and blue cheese in a large bowl.

5 Whisk the oils, vinegar and shallot in small bowl then season to taste with salt and pepper.

6 Drizzle the dressing over the salad and toss thoroughly. Serve immediately.

Serves 6 • Preparation 20 minutes

Gingered almond broccoli salad with cellophane noodles

1 tablespoon peanut oil
2 in/5cm piece fresh ginger, grated
1 small hot red chilli, very finely sliced
4 cloves garlic, minced
4 spring onions, sliced
1 lb/500g broccoli florets, trimmed
10 fresh shiitake mushrooms, sliced
7 oz/200g baby corn
3 tablespoons soy sauce
3 tablespoons mirin
2 tablespoons rice vinegar

1 cos lettuce, shredded
4 oz/125g blanched almonds, toasted

Noodles
3½ oz/100g dried cellophane noodles
2 tablespoons fish sauce
2 tablespoons rice vinegar
2 tablespoons mirin
1 teaspoon palm or brown sugar
½ cup fresh coriander, chopped

1 First, prepare the noodles. Fill a deep jug or bowl with very warm water and soak the cellophane noodles for about 10 minutes or until they are soft and tender. Drain. Mix together the fish sauce, rice vinegar, mirin and sugar then toss through the cellophane noodles. Add the coriander, mix well and set aside.

2 Heat the peanut oil in a wok and add the ginger, chilli, garlic and spring onions and toss thoroughly until the spring onions have wilted, about 3 minutes.

3 Add the broccoli florets and toss well until bright green. Add the mushrooms and corn and continue tossing over a high heat. Add the soy, mirin and rice vinegar and continue cooking for 1 minute.

4 Add the noodles and mix well then remove the pan from the heat.

5 Divide the shredded lettuce amongst the serving plates then top with the broccoli noodle mixture. Garnish with toasted almonds and extra chopped coriander.

When you buy heads of broccoli, trim each little head of broccoli from the main stem – this is called a floret.

Serves 6–8 • Preparation 25 minutes • Cooking 8 minutes

Cabbage and Chinese noodle salad

½ Chinese cabbage
4 baby bok choy
8 spring onions
½ bunch fresh coriander
¾ cup flaked almonds, toasted
½ cup pine nuts, toasted
3½ oz/100g fried Chinese noodles

Dressing
4 tablespoons peanut oil
2 tablespoons balsamic vinegar
2 tablespoons fresh lime or lemon juice
1 tablespoon brown sugar
1 tablespoon soy sauce
salt and freshly ground black pepper

1 Finely shred the cabbage and transfer to a large mixing bowl. Thoroughly wash the bok choy then slice them crosswise and add to the cabbage.
2 Wash the spring onions then slice finely on the diagonal, and add these to the cabbage mixture together with the washed and roughly chopped coriander.
3 Under the griller or in a dry frying pan, toast the almonds and pine nuts and set aside to cool.
4 Mix the nuts and noodles with the cabbage salad.
5 To make the dressing, whisk all the ingredients together with a whisk until thick. Drizzle over the salad and toss thoroughly then serve immediately.

Serves 4 • Preparation 10 minutes • Cooking 5 minutes

Favourite Caesar salad

2 cloves garlic, minced
6 tablespoons olive oil
9 anchovies
juice 1½ lemons
good dash of Worcestershire sauce
½ teaspoon mustard
1–2 tablespoons white wine vinegar
4 eggs, boiled for 1 minute
2 thick slices country bread
salt and freshly ground black pepper
3½ oz/100g prosciutto
3 heads Romaine or cos lettuce
1½ oz/45g Parmesan, shaved

1 Preheat the oven to 440°F/220°C.
2 In a large mixing bowl, place the minced garlic and 4 tablespoons olive oil and, using the base of a metal spoon, pound the garlic into the oil. Add the anchovies and mash these into the oil mixture. Whisk in the lemon juice, Worcestershire sauce, mustard and white wine vinegar, mixing thoroughly to incorporate each ingredient before the next is added.
3 Crack the eggs carefully after they have been boiled for 1 minute then discard the whites and add the yolks to the mixing bowl. Mix these in thoroughly, incorporating them into the other ingredients. Set aside.
4 Cut the bread into cubes and toss with the remaining olive oil and salt and pepper. Transfer to a baking tray and bake the cubes until golden, about 15 minutes. Cool.
5 Crisp the prosciutto in a frying pan then break into smaller pieces.
6 Place the well-washed lettuce leaves in a mixing bowl and toss them thoroughly in the egg yolk mixture for several minutes until all the leaves have been coated. Add the bread cubes and Parmesan and finish with black pepper and crisp prosciutto. Serve immediately.

Serves 6 • Preparation 15 minutes • Cooking 20 minutes

Tortilla salad Mexicana

vegetable oil for frying
4 corn tortillas, cut into strips
3 cups thinly sliced green cabbage
3 cups thinly sliced iceberg lettuce
1 mango, peeled and diced
2–3 jícama. peeled and sliced
1 red onion, finely diced
3 red capsicums, roasted, peeled and
  sliced
½ cup shelled pumpkin seeds, toasted
½ bunch coriander, chopped
salt and freshly ground black pepper

Dressing
1 small mango, peeled and diced
½ cup grapefruit juice
¼ cup fresh lime juice
1–2 small red chillies
4 French shallots, chopped
1½ tablespoons vegetable oil
1 clove garlic

1 To make the dressing, place all the ingredients in a blender or food processor and blend until smooth. Set aside.
2 Next, make the salad. Heat oil in a heavy medium saucepan over medium-high heat. Add a handful of tortilla strips and cook until crisp, about 4 minutes per batch, then remove from the oil and drain on absorbent paper.
3 Combine cabbage, lettuce, mango, jícama, onion, capsicum, pumpkin seeds and coriander in a large bowl. Toss with enough dressing to coat, adding salt and pepper to taste. Add the tortilla and serve.

Jícama is a Mexican turnip.

Serves 4–6 • Preparation 20 minutes • Cooking 5 minutes

Armenian stuffed tomato salad

8 large, round tomatoes
4 tablespoons olive oil
1 large onion, finely chopped
1 large leek, white part only, finely chopped
3 cups cooked white or brown rice
½ cup toasted pine nuts
¾ cup currants
½ cup parsley, chopped
¼ cup fresh mint, chopped
¾ teaspoon sea salt
½ teaspoon freshly ground black pepper
2 cloves garlic, peeled and smashed
½ cup vegetable stock
½ cup white wine
1 lb/500g baby spinach leaves

1 Preheat oven to 360°F/180°C. With a sharp knife, slice the tops off the tomatoes and scoop out as much flesh as possible without damaging the exterior of the tomato. Chop the tomato pulp finely.

2 Heat the olive oil and cook the chopped onion and leek until slightly golden. Add the rice, tomato pulp, nuts, currants, parsley, mint, salt and pepper and sauté until the mixture is hot and well flavoured.

3 Fill each tomato with the rice mixture and replace the tops of the tomatoes. Combine the garlic, stock and white wine and drizzle around tomatoes, then bake for 15 minutes.

4 Meanwhile, wash and dry the spinach leaves. When the tomatoes have finished cooking, remove them and toss the remaining hot liquid through the spinach, discarding the garlic.

5 Place a mound of warm spinach on each plate and perch a tomato on top. Drizzle any remaining liquid over and serve.

Serves 8 • Preparation 20 minutes • Cooking 20 minutes

Turkish tabouli

¾ cup fine bulgar wheat
½ bunch spring onions, trimmed and
  finely sliced
1 large ripe tomato, deseeded and diced
½ red capsicum, deseeded and diced
1 small cucumber, peeled, deseeded
  and diced
1 cup parsley, finely chopped
¼ cup fresh mint, sliced
2 tablespoons Turkish red capsicum paste
  (see below)

juice of 1 lemon
3 tablespoons olive oil
½ tablespoon pomegranate molasses
2 teaspoons ground cumin
salt and freshly ground black pepper

Turkish red capsicum paste
2 red capsicums, flesh only
2 hot red chillies
½ teaspoon salt
½ teaspoon sugar
2 teaspoons olive oil

1 To make the Turkish red capsicum paste, place the capsicums, chillies, salt, sugar and olive oil in a food processor with 1 tablespoon water and process until smooth. Transfer the mixture to a saucepan and simmer gently until the mixture is thick and the liquid has reduced, about 1 hour, stirring frequently. Cool.

2 Cover the bulgar with cool water and allow to stand for 30 minutes. Drain well, squeezing out any excess water. In a mixing bowl, combine the bulgar, spring onions, tomato, capsicum, cucumber, parsley and mint and mix well. Add the red capsicum paste and mix thoroughly until the salad takes on a lovely red hue.

3 Whisk together the lemon juice, olive oil, pomegranate molasses, cumin and salt and pepper. Pour the dressing over the vegetable mixture and toss thoroughly to make sure all the ingredients are coated. Add extra salt to taste, if necessary, then chill for 2 hours. Serve cold or at room temperature.

Serves 4 • Preparation 40 minutes • Cooking 1 hour

Sweet potato chip salad

2 lb/900g sweet potatoes, thinly sliced
3–4 tablespoons olive oil
6 oz/170g baby English spinach leaves
6 oz/170g rocket leaves
3 tomatoes, chopped
2 red onions, sliced
4 tablespoons pitted black olives
2 oz/60g Parmesan, shaved

Sweet oregano dressing
¼ cup fresh oregano leaves
1½ tablespoons brown sugar
⅓ cup balsamic vinegar
freshly ground black pepper

1 Preheat a barbecue to a high heat. Brush the sweet potatoes with oil and cook in batches on the barbecue plate for 4 minutes each side or until golden and crisp. Drain on absorbent paper.

2 Place the spinach, rocket, tomatoes, onions, olives and cheese in a bowl and toss to combine. Cover and chill until required.

3 To make the dressing, place the oregano, sugar, vinegar and pepper to taste in a screw-top jar and shake to combine.

4 To serve, add the sweet potato chips to the salad, drizzle with the dressing and toss to combine.

Serves 8 • Preparation 40 minutes • Cooking 10 minutes

Grilled brie with beetroot salad

1 avocado
8 oz/250g cooked beetroots, drained and chopped
2 stalks celery, sliced
1 red dessert apple, cored and chopped
4 slices stonebaked white bread
4 oz/125g Dutch Brie, quartered
4 oz/125g mixed salad leaves

Dressing
3 tablespoons extra virgin olive oil
3 tablespoons cider vinegar
1 clove garlic, crushed
1 small red onion, finely chopped
1 tablespoon tomato purée
sea salt and freshly ground black pepper

1 Peel and slice the avocado and place in a bowl together with the beetroots, celery and apple. Cover and set aside. Preheat the grill to high and lightly toast the bread for 2–3 minutes each side. Place a slice of Brie on top of each toast, then return them to the grill. Cook until the cheese is melted and slightly golden.

2 Meanwhile, make the dressing. Place all the ingredients in a small saucepan and bring to the boil. Simmer for 2–3 minutes, until warmed through.

3 To serve, divide the salad leaves between 4 plates, top with the beetroot mixture and place a cheese toast on each plate. Drizzle over the warm dressing and serve immediately.

Serves 4 • Preparation 15 minutes • Cooking 10 minutes

Anchovy, egg and Parmesan salad

2 medium eggs
2 heads chicory
2 lettuces, leaves torn
8 anchovy fillets in oil, drained and cut in half lengthwise
1 tablespoon capers, drained
2 cherry tomatoes, halved
2 oz/60g Parmesan, shaved
2 tablespoons extra virgin olive oil
juice of 1 lemon
salt and freshly ground black pepper
¼ cup flat-leaf parsley

1 Bring a small saucepan of water to the boil, add the eggs and boil for 10 minutes. Remove from the pan, cool under cold running water, then shell. Cut each egg lengthwise into quarters.

2 On each serving plate, arrange 8 alternating chicory and lettuce leaves, tips facing outwards, in a star shape. Place 2 egg quarters on the base of 2 opposite lettuce leaves, then place 2 anchovy halves on the other 2 opposite lettuce leaves. Scatter the capers over the leaves.

3 Put a cherry tomato half in the centre of each plate and drape 2 anchovy halves over the top. Top with Parmesan, then drizzle over the olive oil and lemon juice. Season to taste and garnish with parsley.

Serves 4 • Preparation 20 minutes • Cooking 10 minutes

Green beans with prosciutto and Parmesan

6 quail eggs
8 oz/250g baby beans, blanched
2 oz/60g prosciutto, sliced
2 oz/60g Parmesan, shaved
freshly ground black pepper
pinch of sea salt

Dressing
2 tablespoons extra virgin olive oil
1 tablespoon white wine vinegar

1 Place quail eggs in a small saucepan of cold water, bring to the boil, and boil for
   3 minutes. Rinse under cold water until eggs are cool, then peel and cut in half.
2 Combine the beans, prosciutto, quail eggs and Parmesan in a bowl. Sprinkle with the
   black pepper and sea salt. Combine the dressing ingredients, drizzle over the salad
   and serve.

Serves 4 • Preparation 10 minutes • Cooking 8 minutes

Tomato and mozzarella salad

6 Roma tomatoes, sliced
8 oz/250g buffalo mozzarella, drained and sliced
2 spring onions, sliced
2½ oz/75g black olives
salt and freshly ground black pepper

Dressing
3 tablespoons extra virgin olive oil
1 clove garlic, crushed
2 teaspoons balsamic vinegar
¼ cup fresh basil, chopped

1 Arrange the tomatoes, mozzarella, spring onions and olives in layers on serving plates and season.
2 To make the dressing, heat the oil and garlic in a small saucepan over a very low heat for 2 minutes or until the garlic has softened but not browned. Remove the pan from the heat, add the vinegar and basil, then pour over the salad.

Serves 4 • Preparation 10 minutes • Cooking 2 minutes

Waldorf salad with red Leicester

6 oz/175g red cabbage, finely shredded
4 stalks celery, sliced
5 oz/150g red Leicester cheese, cut into ½ in/12mm cubes
2½ oz/75g seedless red grapes, halved
2 red apples, cored and chopped
1 romaine lettuce, leaves torn
½ teaspoon poppy seeds

Dressing
5 oz/150g natural yoghurt
2 tablespoons mayonnaise
1 teaspoon fresh lemon juice or white wine vinegar
freshly ground black pepper

1 To make the dressing, mix together the yoghurt, mayonnaise, lemon juice or vinegar and seasoning. In a large bowl, combine the cabbage, celery, red Leicester, grapes and apples, then toss with the dressing.

2 Divide the lettuce leaves between plates and top with the cabbage and cheese mixture. Sprinkle with poppy seeds before serving.

Serves 4 • Preparation 8 minutes

Beetroot, pear and bitter-leaf salad

2 oz/60g walnut pieces
7 oz/200g mixed salad leaves, including radicchio and frisée
8 oz/250g cooked beetroot slices
2 pears, quartered, cored, sliced
1 oz/30g Parmesan, grated
fresh chives

Dressing
½ cup fresh herbs, including basil, chives, mint and parsley, chopped
4 tablespoons walnut oil
2 tablespoons extra virgin olive oil
1 clove garlic, crushed
2 teaspoons red wine vinegar
1 teaspoon clear honey
salt and freshly ground black pepper

1 Preheat the grill to high. To make the dressing, blend the herbs, walnut oil, olive oil, garlic, vinegar and honey until smooth in a food processor or with a hand blender. Season to taste.

2 Place the walnuts on a baking sheet and grill for 2–3 minutess until golden, turning often. Arrange the leaves, beetroot and pear slices on serving plates. Scatter over the walnuts, then shave over thin slivers of Parmesan using a vegetable peeler. Spoon the dressing over the salad and garnish with whole chives.

Serves 4 • Preparation 15 minutes • Cooking 15 minutes

Broad beans with coriander

3 cups shelled broad beans
8 slices prosciutto
1 small red onion, thinly sliced
2 tablespoons extra virgin olive oil
1 tablespoon white wine vinegar
½ teaspoon sugar
¼ cup fresh coriander, chopped
4 sprigs fresh flat-leaf parsley, chopped
salt and freshly ground black pepper

1 Cook broad beans in a saucepan of boiling water for 1 minute. Drain and rinse under cold water. Remove skins from the beans and discard.
2 Place prosciutto on a baking tray and place under a hot grill. Cook for 1–2 minutes each side or until crisp. When cool, break into pieces.
3 Place broad beans, prosciutto and onion in a serving bowl. Drizzle over extra virgin olive oil and white wine vinegar. Sprinkle with sugar, coriander and parsley and season with salt and pepper. Toss well to combine.

Serves 4 • Preparation 20 minutes • Cooking 10 minutes

Mixed salad

1 red capsicum, deseeded and cut into quarters
3 vine-ripened tomatoes, cut into wedges
1 tablespoon olive oil
1 small cucumber, sliced
1 small red onion, finely chopped
½ cup black olives
5 oz/150g mixed green leaves such as curly endive, baby spinach, butter lettuce and
   watercress
¼ cup fresh coriander leaves

Dressing
¼ cup olive oil
1 tablespoon lemon juice
1 tablespoon red wine vinegar
½ teaspoon sugar
salt and freshly ground black pepper

1 Place capsicum on a baking tray and place under a hot grill for 6–8 minutes or until
   skin is blistered and black. Leave to cool. Remove skin and thinly slice.
2 Preheat oven to 360°F/180°C. Place tomatoes on a baking tray lined with baking
   paper. Lightly spray or brush with olive oil and season with salt and pepper. Bake for
   15–20 minutes or until just soft. Set aside.
3 Combine capsicums, tomatoes, cucumber, red onion, olives, salad leaves and
   coriander in a large serving bowl.
4 Combine ingredients for dressing in a small jug. Pour dressing over salad and toss to
   combine.

Serves 4 • Preparation 25 minutes • Cooking 25 minutes

Baby spinach, feta, artichoke and walnut salad

1 red capsicum, quartered and seeded
1 tablespoon olive oil
3½ oz/100g walnuts
7 oz/200g baby spinach, washed
7 oz/200g Greek feta, cubed
10 oz/300g artichoke hearts, quartered
½ cup black olives, pitted

Dressing
½ cup extra virgin olive oil
¼ cup lemon juice
2 teaspoons honey
4 sprigs oregano, leaves removed and chopped
freshly ground black pepper

1 Preheat grill. Place capsicum under grill and cook until it turns black on top. Cut into strips and set aside.

2 In a small jar, combine all ingredients for dressing and shake well.

3 In a frying pan, heat the olive oil, add walnuts, and cook for 1–2 minutes. In a large salad bowl, combine baby spinach, feta, artichoke hearts and olives, then drizzle dressing over ingredients. Serve with pita bread.

Serves 4–6 • Preparation 20 minutes • Cooking 16 minutes

Celeriac and herb remoulade

2 medium eggs
1 lb/500g celeriac, grated
2 tablespoons olive oil
1 tablespoon sesame oil
juice of 1 lemon
¼ cup fresh parsley, chopped
½ small bunch fresh chives, chopped
salt and freshly ground black pepper

1 Bring a saucepan of water to the boil. Add the eggs and boil for 10 minutes. Cool under cold running water, then remove the shells and finely chop the eggs.
2 Place the celeriac and chopped eggs in a large bowl. Mix together the olive oil, sesame oil and lemon juice and pour over the celeriac and eggs. Add the parsley, chives and seasoning, then mix thoroughly.

Serves 4 • Preparation 15 minutes • Cooking 15 minutes

fruit
salads

Fruit salad makes a refreshing, healthy and light dessert that few people can resist. The ways in which you can present fresh or canned fruit are almost endless. This chapter presents a selection of fruit salads that you will be proud to serve at any meal for any occasion.

Vietnamese green papaya salad

Salad
1½ lb/750g green papaya
4 spring onions, very finely julienned
½ white radish, very finely julienned
12 leaves Asian mint, chopped
12 leaves Thai basil, chopped
¼ bunch coriander, leaves only
1 clove garlic, minced
2 tablespoons dried shrimp or crushed peanuts

Dressing
½ teaspoon shrimp paste
3 tablespoons rice vinegar
3 tablespoons lime juice
2 tablespoons fish sauce
2 tablespoons sugar
1 tablespoon sweet chilli sauce

1 Finely julienne the papaya and toss with the finely julienned spring onions, white radish, chopped fresh herbs and garlic.

2 To make the dressing, dilute the shrimp paste in 2 tablespoons boiling water, then whisk with all other dressing ingredients. If the sauce is a little too acidic, add a little extra water as required to dilute the flavour to your taste. Continue whisking until the dressing is well mixed.

3 Toss the dressing through the papaya mixture, taking care to disperse the dressing thoroughly. Scatter over the dried shrimp or peanuts to serve.

Serves 8 • Preparation 15 mins

Avocado, mango and papaya salad

2 ripe avocados
juice of ½ lime
2 papayas
2 oz/60g mixed salad leaves
fresh coriander

Dressing
1 ripe mango
1 tablespoon rice wine vinegar or 1 teaspoon white wine vinegar
juice of 1 lime
½ teaspoon sesame oil
½ in/12mm piece fresh ginger, finely chopped
½ teaspoon clear honey

1 To make the dressing, peel the mango, slice the flesh off the stone, then chop roughly. In a food processor, blend to a thin purée with the vinegar, lime juice, oil, ginger and honey. Alternatively, press the mango flesh through a sieve, then mix with the other dressing ingredients.

2 Halve and peel the avocados, discarding the stones, then finely slice lengthwise. Toss in the lime juice to stop them turning brown.

3 Halve the papayas, then scoop out and discard the seeds. Peel and finely slice the flesh. Arrange with the avocado and salad leaves on serving plates. Pour over the dressing and garnish with coriander.

Serves 4 • Preparation 20 minutes

Citrus fruit salad with ginger

1 pink grapefruit
1 large orange
1 tangerine, peeled and divided into segments
zest of 1 lime, cut into matchsticks
2 oz/60g cumquats, halved, pips removed
juice of 1 small lemon
5 oz/150mL ginger beer
3 tablespoons caster sugar
2 pieces preserved ginger in syrup, finely chopped
fresh mint

1 Slice the tops and bottoms off the grapefruit and orange using a sharp serrated knife – hold the fruit over a bowl to catch the juices. Cut down the side of the fruits, following the curves, to remove the skin and pith. Cut out the segments, leaving the membranes behind. Place in a serving dish with the tangerine segments. Reserve the fruit juices.

2 Place the lime zest and cumquats in a saucepan with 150mL water. Simmer for 10 minutes or until softened. Add the cumquats to the other fruit and drain the lime zest on absorbent paper. Reserve the liquid.

3 Add the lemon juice, ginger beer, sugar and any juices from the fruit to the reserved cooking liquid. Heat gently, stirring, for 5 minutes or until the sugar dissolves. Pour the mixture over the fruit and stir in the chopped ginger. Sprinkle over the lime zest and garnish with fresh mint.

You can use whichever citrus fruits you like in this dessert, but don't leave out the lime – its flavour and colour make all the difference.

Serves 4 • Preparation 20 minutes • Cooking 15 minutes

Oriental fruit salad

3 stalks lemongrass
2 oz/60g caster sugar
1 small rock melon
1 mango
14 oz/400g canned lychees, drained
fresh mint leaves

1 Peel outer layers from lemongrass stalks, finely chop lower white bulbous parts and discard fibrous tops. Place lemongrass, sugar and 100mL water in a saucepan. Simmer, stirring, for 5 minutes or until the sugar dissolves, then bring to the boil. Remove from the heat and leave to cool for 20 minutes. Refrigerate for 30 minutes.

2 Halve melon and scrape out seeds. Cut into wedges, then remove skin and cut flesh into small chunks. Slice off the 2 fat sides of the mango close to the stone. Cut a criss-cross pattern across the flesh (but not through the skin) of each piece, then push the skin inside out to expose the cubes of flesh and cut them off.

3 Place melon, mango and lychees in serving bowls. Strain lemongrass syrup and pour over the fruit. Garnish with mint and serve.

Serves 4 • Preparation 50 minutes • Cooking 25 minutes

Fresh fruit salad

2 oranges
2–3 tablespoons fresh, unsweetened orange juice
1 red apple, cored but not peeled, cut into 1cm pieces
1 pear, cored, peeled and cut into 1cm pieces
2 oz/60g seedless grapes
1 ripe nectarine, skinned, stoned and cut into chunks
1 banana
6 strawberries
½ cup natural yoghurt

1 Slice the top and bottom off each orange and place on a work surface. Using a serrated knife, cut off the skin and pith, following the curve of the fruit. Holding the oranges over a bowl, cut between the membranes to release the segments. Put the segments into a large serving bowl with the orange juice.

2 Add the apple, pear, grapes and nectarine to the bowl and mix gently but thoroughly so that the orange juice coats the fruit (this will stop the fruit discolouring). Put the fruit salad in the refrigerator and chill for 1 hour to allow the flavours to develop.

3 Just before serving, peel the banana, slice thinly and add to the bowl. Remove the green hulls from the strawberries, cut in half and add to the bowl. Mix gently and divide between 4 serving bowls. Top each with yoghurt and serve..

Serves 4 • Preparation 1hour 20 mins

Waldorf salad

1 green apple, cut into chunks
1 red apple, cut into chunks
1 stalk celery, sliced
5 baby cos leaves, finely shredded
¼ cup mayonnaise
1 teaspoon lemon juice
¼ cup pecan or walnut halves

1 Combine the apples, celery and lettuce in a bowl with the mayonnaise, lemon juice
   and pecans or walnuts. Mix well and serve.

Serves 4 • Preparation 5 minutes

Fruit and nut salad

2 red apples, chopped
2 stalks celery, sliced
8 oz/250g strawberries, halved
3 tablespoons sultanas
2 oz/60g chopped pecans

Dressing
4 sprigs fresh mint, finely chopped
3 tablespoons natural yoghurt
2 tablespoons lemon juice
freshly ground black pepper

1 Place apples, celery, strawberries, sultanas and pecans in a salad bowl.
2 To make dressing, place mint, yoghurt, lemon juice and black pepper to taste in a
   bowl and stir to combine.
3 Spoon dressing over salad and toss to combine. Cover and refrigerate until required.

Serves 4 • Preparation 8 minutes

Fruit salad in spicy lime syrup

½ pineapple, diced
1 mango, diced
1 papaya, diced
1 apple, cored and diced
1 cucumber, peeled and diced
12 rambutans, peeled and deseeded

Syrup
1 cup brown sugar
grated zest of 1 lime
2 tablespoons lime juice
1 teaspoon tamarind paste
1 medium-sized chilli, deseeded and finely chopped

1 Combine sugar, lime zest and juice with ½ cup water in a small saucepan to make the syrup. Bring to the boil and simmer over low heat for 8–10 minutes and allow to cool. Add tamarind paste and chilli and stir to combine.
2 Combine fruit in a serving bowl. Pour over syrup and toss before serving.

Serves 4 • Preparation 10 minutes • Cooking 10 minutes

favourite dressings

An interesting dressing is all that is needed to turn a simple salad into something special. In this chapter you will find a selection of dressing recipes to suit all tastes and salad combinations. A good oil and a well-flavoured vinegar are the basis of many good dressings. Sometimes lemon or lime juice will replace vinegar to make a deliciously refreshing dressing.

Real home-made herb mayonnaise

10oz/300mL olive oil
10 oz/300mL grapeseed oil
2 cups fresh herbs of your choice, for example
  parsley, chives, basil, chervil
2 cloves garlic, peeled
2 eggs, plus 2 egg yolks
1 tablespoon Dijon mustard
1 tablespoon white wine vinegar
salt and freshly ground black pepper

1 Combine the olive and grapeseed oils and
   set aside. Process the herbs and garlic until
   chopped and set aside.
2 Place the eggs and egg yolks in a food
   processor and process for 2 minutes. While
   processing, add the mustard and half the
   vinegar and then add the oil mixture in a
   thin stream. When most of the oil has been
   used, stop the processor and add the herb
   mixture, remaining vinegar and remaining
   oil and process briefly to combine. Add salt
   and pepper to taste and chill until ready
   to use. *Store in the refrigerator. Goes with
   everything*. **Makes about 3 cups**

Yoghurt dressing

2 tablespoons snipped fresh chives
1 clove garlic, crushed
¾ cup natural yoghurt
2 tablespoons white wine vinegar

1 Place chives, garlic, yoghurt and vinegar in
   a bowl and whisk to combine. *Very versatile
   and a great vegetarian favourite.*
   Makes 1 cup

Coriander chilli mayonnaise

1 small fresh red chilli
1 large bunch fresh coriander
3 tablespoons sour cream
3 tablespoons natural yoghurt
2 cloves garlic, chopped
6 mint leaves
juice and zest of 1 lime
salt and freshly ground black pepper

1 Remove and discard the seeds of the chilli
   and wash and dry the coriander.
2 Place the sour cream, yoghurt, garlic, mint,
   chilli and coriander in a food processor and
   process until smooth. Add the lime juice and
   zest and process briefly, then add salt and
   pepper to taste. *Goes well with flaked cold
   salmon, warm boiled baby potatoes, avocado
   and asparagus.*
   Makes about ½ cup

Mint yoghurt dressing

2 tablespoons snipped fresh chives
1 clove garlic, crushed
¾ cup natural yoghurt
2 tablespoons white wine vinegar
¼ cup fresh mint, finely chopped

1 Place chives, garlic, yoghurt, vinegar and
   fresh mint in a bowl and whisk to combine.
   *Another vegetarian favourite with an added
   hit of mint freshness.* **Makes 1 cup**

Blue cheese mayonnaise

¼ teaspoon dry mustard
2 egg yolks
1 cup olive oil
2 tablespoons lemon juice or white wine
  vinegar
freshly ground black pepper
3 oz/90g blue cheese, crumbled

1 Place mustard and egg yolks in a food
   processor or blender and process until just
   combined. With machine running, gradually
   pour in oil and process until mixture
   thickens. Blend in lemon juice or vinegar and
   black pepper to taste. Add the blue cheese
   and process to combine. *Very rich and old-
   fashioned, great with witlof.* **Makes 1½ cups**

Thousand island
yoghurt dressing

2 tablespoons snipped fresh chives
¾ cup natural yoghurt
2 tablespoons white wine vinegar
2 tablespoons green olives, chopped
2 spring onions, finely chopped
1 hard-boiled egg, chopped
1 tablespoon finely chopped green capsicum
1 tablespoon tomato paste
½ teaspoon chilli sauce

1 Place all ingredients into a bowl and whisk
   to combine. *Store dressing in a screw-top jar
   in the refrigerator for up to 1 week.*
   Makes 1 cup

Oriental mayonnaise

2 tablespoons soft brown sugar
fresh ginger 2cm piece, grated
1 teaspoon fennel seeds
1 clove garlic, crushed
⅓ cup soy sauce
2 tablespoons cider vinegar
2 egg yolks
½ teaspoon dry mustard
¾ cup vegetable oil
2 teaspoons sesame oil
½ teaspoon hot chilli sauce

1 Place sugar, ginger, fennel seeds, garlic,
   soy sauce and vinegar in a saucepan and
   bring to the boil. Reduce heat and simmer,
   uncovered, for 5 minutes or until mixture
   reduces by half. Remove from heat, strain
   and discard fennel seeds. Set aside to cool.

2 Place egg yolks and mustard in a food
   processor or blender and process until just
   combined. With machine running, gradually
   pour in vegetable and sesame oils and
   process until mayonnaise thickens.

3 Add soy mixture and process to combine.
   Mix in chilli sauce to taste. *Store mayonnaise
   in a jar or bottle in the refrigerator for up to
   1 week.* **Makes about 1½ cups**

Turkish hazelnut and garlic dressing

2 slices peasant-style white bread, crusts removed
6 oz/180g toasted hazelnuts
3 cloves garlic, minced
zest and juice of 1 lemon
1 tablespoon white wine vinegar
½ cup olive oil
3 tablespoons natural yoghurt
pinch of sea salt

1   Toast the bread until golden then tear into small pieces and place in a food processor and process until crumbs form. Add the hazelnuts, garlic and lemon zest and process until the nuts are well crushed then, with the motor running, add the lemon juice, vinegar and olive oil.

2   Finally, add the yoghurt and process briefly. Season to taste then set aside. *Goes well with shellfish and cold poached salmon, boiled cool potatoes, blanched green beans and crisp vegetables.* **Makes about 1 cup**

Basic vinaigrette

¾ cup olive oil
¼ cup cider vinegar
1 tablespoon Dijon mustard
freshly ground black pepper

1   Place oil, vinegar, mustard and black pepper to taste in a screw-top jar and shake well to combine. *The foundation of many great salads where the freshness of the ingredients only need simple embellishment.* **Makes 1 cup**

Indonesian satay sauce

2 tablespoons peanut oil
5 cloves garlic, minced
½ small red chilli, minced
5 tablespoons peanut butter
1½ tablespoons tomato paste
3 tablespoons hoisin sauce
1 teaspoon sugar
1 teaspoon fish sauce
¼ cup peanuts, crushed

1   Heat the oil and sauté the garlic and minced chilli until softened, about 2 minutes, then add all remaining ingredients and ¾ cup water and whisk while heating. Bring to the boil and simmer until thickened slightly, about 3 minutes. *Goes well with cold sliced chicken or lamb and crisp noodles with crunchy Asian vegetables, like bok choy.* **Makes about 1 cup**

Curried yoghurt dressing

2 tablespoons snipped fresh chives
1 clove garlic, crushed
¾ cup natural yoghurt
2 tablespoons white wine vinegar
1 teaspoon curry powder
dash of chilli sauce

1   Place chives, garlic, yoghurt, vinegar, curry powder and chilli sauce in a bowl and whisk to combine. *A time-honoured favourite of the British.* **Makes 1 cup**

Roasted garlic vinaigrette

1 large bulb garlic
1 tablespoon olive oil
3 tablespoons balsamic vinegar
2 teaspoons extra virgin olive oil
1 teaspoon Dijon mustard
salt and freshly ground black pepper

1 Separate the garlic cloves but do not peel.
   Toss them with the olive oil and place in a
   small ovenproof baking dish. Bake at 220°C
   for 20–30 minutes until the cloves are golden
   brown. Remove from the oven and cool.

2 When the cloves are cool enough to handle,
   thoroughly squeeze the soft roasted garlic
   out of each clove, discarding the skins. Purée
   the garlic with 3 tablespoons boiling water,
   the balsamic vinegar, extra virgin olive oil
   and mustard, adding salt and pepper to
   taste. *Goes well with potato salads, salad of
   green beans with toasted nuts, fresh tuna or
   salmon.* **Makes approximately ¾ cup**

Ginger and soy dressing

2 in/5cm fresh ginger
1 clove garlic, crushed
½ cup soy sauce
1 tablespoon cider vinegar
1 tablespoon sesame oil

1 Place ginger, garlic, soy sauce, ½ cup water,
   the vinegar and oil in a screw-top jar and
   shake well to combine. Stand for at least
   15 minutes before using. *Store dressing
   in the jar in which you made it, in the
   refrigerator for 2–3 weeks. Shake well and
   bring to room temperature before using.*
   Makes 1 cup

Fresh parsley vinaigrette

1 bunch fresh flat-leaf parsley
6 tablespoons red wine vinegar
2 cloves garlic
1 cup olive oil
salt and freshly ground black pepper

1 Wash and dry the parsley. Place the parsley
   in a food processor with the vinegar and
   garlic and process until the parsley is well
   chopped.

2 With the mixer running, add the olive oil
   in a thin stream and continue processing
   until the dressing is thick. Season with
   salt and pepper to taste and use at room
   temperature. *Goes well with roasted Italian
   vegetables, baby rocket leaves with croutons
   and Parmesan shavings, salads of summer
   tomatoes, basil and olives.* **Makes 1½ cups**

Japanese ginger miso vinaigrette

4 tablespoons rice vinegar
1 tablespoon miso paste
2cm piece fresh ginger, minced
1 large clove garlic, minced
2 tablespoons toasted sesame seeds
6 fresh basil leaves, finely sliced
¼ teaspoon dried red chilli flakes
3½ oz/100mL peanut oil

1 Whisk together the rice vinegar, miso,
   minced ginger, minced garlic, toasted
   sesame seeds and basil with the chilli flakes,
   then slowly whisk in the oil a little at a time
   until it has all been added. *Goes well with
   oven-roasted eggplant, hokkien noodles and
   Asian stir-fried vegetables.* **Makes 1 cup**

Chinese ginger hoisin vinaigrette

3 tablespoons hoisin sauce
3 tablespoons white wine vinegar
3 tablespoons chicken stock
1 tablespoon peanut oil
1 tablespoon toasted sesame oil
1 tablespoon minced or grated fresh ginger
1 tablespoon soy sauce
2 teaspoons mustard of your choice
pinch of salt

1   Purée all ingredients in a food processor until smooth, then add salt to taste if desired. Use immediately or store in the refrigerator for up to 1 week. Allow to come back to room temperature then whisk thoroughly before using. *Goes well with blanched asparagus, Asian noodle salads, salads with thinly sliced beef and Asian vegetables and herbs*. **Makes approximately 1 cup**

Warm shallot and lemon dressing

4 large French shallots
2 cloves garlic
3 tablespoons vegetable oil
juice of 2 lemons
zest of 1 lemon
3 tablespoons vegetable stock
salt and freshly ground black pepper

1   Peel and mince the shallots and garlic. Heat the oil in a small frying pan until smoking, then add the shallots and garlic and sauté until translucent, about 5 minutes.

2   Whisk in the lemon juice, lemon zest and vegetable stock. Add salt and pepper to taste and simmer briefly. Remove from the heat and allow to cool slightly before using. *Goes well with baby spinach or rocket, fresh tomatoes, sliced or quartered, cold poached chicken or other poultry.*
Makes approximately ¾ cup

Vietnamese lime, chilli and herb dressing

4 tablespoons fish sauce
4 tablespoons fresh lime juice
2 tablespoons palm sugar
2 small hot red chillies
6 cloves garlic
⅔ oz/20g piece fresh ginger, peeled

1   Whisk together the fish sauce, lime juice, 3 tablespoons water and the palm sugar until the sugar has dissolved. Finely mince the chillies with the garlic cloves and ginger then whisk in the liquid. Allow the flavours to blend for 5 minutes then toss with your salad. *Goes well with all types of Asian noodles, warm salads with thinly sliced beef, water chestnuts, salads of shellfish mixed with Asian greens.*
Makes approximately 1 cup

Index

American potato salad 179

Anchovy, egg and Parmesan salad 212

Armenian stuffed tomato salad 204

Artichokes la polita 156

Asian chicken bok choy salad 59

Asian gingered coleslaw 183

Asparagus and baby green beans with hazelnut dressing 132

Asparagus and tomato salad with cucumber 147

Avocado, mango and papaya salad 235

Baby octopus salad 48

Baby spinach, feta, artichoke and walnut salad 227

Baby spinach, toasted pine nut and avocado salad 176

Barbecued seafood salad 40

Barley, feta and pear salad 129

Basic vinaigrette 252

Bean and artichoke salad 117

Beetroot, pear and bitter-leaf salad 220

Blue cheese mayonnaise 251

Broad beans with coriander 223

Bulgar wheat salad with grilled capsicums 113

Cabbage and Chinese noodle salad 199

Calabrian salad 135

Caramelised ocean trout salad with cellophane noodles 16

Celeriac and herb remoulade 228

Celery, carrot and apple salad with tahini 148

Chicken and avocado salad 83

Chicken grape salad 71

Chickpea and trout salad 24

Chinese ginger hoisin vinaigrette 254

Citrus fruit salad with ginger 236

Coriander chilli mayonnaise 250

Curried yoghurt dressing 252

Favourite Caesar salad 200

Fijian kokoda 12

Fresh fruit salad 240

Fresh parsley vinaigrette 253

Fruit and nut salad 244

Fruit salad in spicy lime syrup 247

Garlic prawn salad 44

Ginger and soy dressing 253

Gingered almond broccoli salad with cellophane noodles 196

Gingered Thai rice salad 101

Greek orzo salad with olives and capsicums 94

Greek salad 192

Green beans with prosciutto and Parmesan 215

Grilled brie with beetroot salad 211

Honeyed calamari salad 27

Indian chickpea salad with spinach 106

Indian salad of spiced chicken and dhal 67

Indonesian satay sauce 252

Insalata caprese 152

Insalata spirale 121

Israeli kumquat chicken salad with mixed wild rice 63

Italian chicken salad 56

Italian sausage with zucchini and mezuma leaves 72

Italian tuna and bean salad 118

Japanese ginger miso vinaigrette 253

Japanese rice noodle salad 86

Lettuce, avocado and peanut salad 164

Lobster and smoked ocean trout salad 31

Marinated bean salad 89

Marinated mushrooms on a bed of leaves 160

Marinated salmon, cucumber and daikon salad 15

Marsala quail salad 64

Mediterranean scallop salad 47

Middle Eastern bean and
artichoke salad 105

Mint yoghurt dressing 250

Mixed salad 224

Mixed shellfish and potato
salad 35

Mushroom and snowpea
salad 144

New Mexico chicken salad 60

Oregano lamb and
couscous salad 76

Oriental fruit salad 239

Oriental mayonnaise 251

Pakistani green bean salad
with coriander and ginger 172

Pasta and asparagus salad 109

Pasta salad with roasted
garlic 98

Peach and prawn entrée
salad 28

Pila di melanzana 155

Prawn and avocado cocktail 32

Real home-made herb
mayonnaise 250

Roasted beetroot, orange
and fennel salad 159

Roasted corn and bean
salad Mexicana 102

Roasted garlic vinaigrette 253

Roasted vegetable salad 167

Salad of sautéed duck with
thyme and honey 55

Salmon and lentil salad 23

Scandinavian mussels 43

Seared scallop salad 20

Sicilian cauliflower salad 168

South American bean salad 93

Spicy wild rice salad 110

Summer greens with lime
and coriander 140

Summer salad of grilled
chicken, spinach and mango 52

Summer tabouli 126

Sweet potato and peanut
salad 175

Sweet potato chip salad 208

Tandoori lamb salad with
black onion seeds and
sesame 68

Thai beef salad 75

Thai calamari salad 19

Thousand island yoghurt
dressing 251

Three bean rice salad 122

Tomato and bread salad
with pesto dressing 184

Tomato and mozzarella
salad 216

Tomato and onion salad
with feta dressing 163

Tortilla salad Mexicana 203

Tuna and lemon fettuccine
salad 39

Tuna barley niçoise 90

Tuna bean salad 36

Turkish hazelnut and garlic
dressing 252

Turkish tabouli 207

Tuscan panzanella with
roasted tomato vinaigrette 136

Vietnamese green papaya
salad 232

Vietnamese herbed
rice noodles with peanuts
and asparagus 114

Vietnamese lime, chilli and
herb dressing 254

Waldorf salad 243

Waldorf salad with red
Leicester 219

Warm duck and mango salad 80

Warm herbed potato salad 143

Warm lima bean and
prosciutto salad with rocket 97

Warm Mediterranean pasta
shell salad 125

Warm salad of capsicum
and rosemary 139

Warm shallot and lemon
dressing 254

Warm spinach salad with
walnuts 171

Warm Thai chicken salad 79

Warm tomato gratin salad 191

Warm vegetable salad with
prosciutto 151

Watercress and pear salad 188

Witlof salad with apples,
blue cheese and pecans 195

Yoghurt dressing 250

Zucchini and hazelnut salad 180